⚡ INSIGHT POCKET

ECUADOR

Discovery CHANNEL

APA PUBLICATIONS L
Part of the Langenscheidt Publishing Group

4

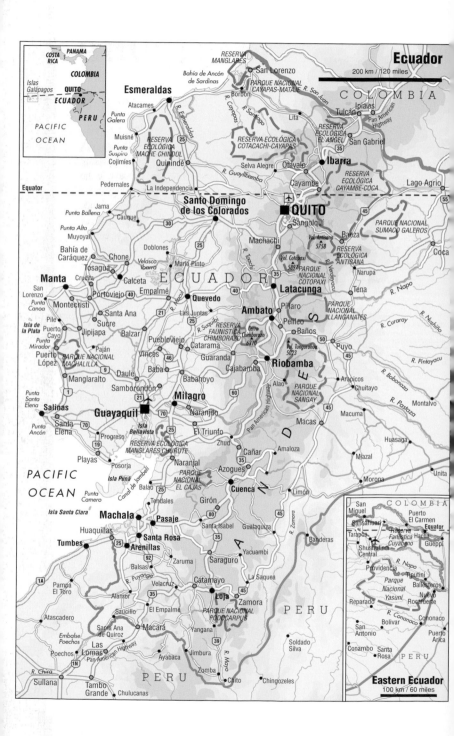

Welcome

This guidebook combines the interests and enthusiasms of two of the world's best-known information providers: Insight Guides, who have set the standard for visual travel guides since 1970, and Discovery Channel, the world's premier source of non-fiction television programing. The guide's aim is to help visitors get the most out of a short stay in Ecuador by using a series of itineraries designed by Peter Frost, Insight Guides' specialist in the region. The tours cover all the must-see sights – the two World Heritage cities of Quito and Cuenca, the equator, Cotopaxi volcano, the Galápagos Islands – but also venture off the beaten path to visit remote highland villages inhabited by indigenous communities, bustling coastal towns near beautiful beaches, market towns where talented artisans produce wonderful craft-work, and fascinating rainforest nature reserves. Supporting the itineraries are sections on history and culture, eating out, shopping and practical inform-ation, including a list of recommended hotels.

Peter Frost, the author of *Insight Pocket Guide Ecuador*, is a writer, photographer and independent scholar who has been exploring the Andes since 1971. He now lives in Peru, where he publishes local guides to exploring Cusco and the Machu Picchu Historical Sanc-tuary; he also wrote *Insight Pocket Guide Peru*. He has traveled in Ecuador since the 1980s, but would like to acknowledge the generous help of those who have traveled further: his friends Jean Brown, George Fletcher and Margarita Goodhart.

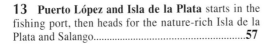

Pages 2/3: ploughing the fields near Ingapirca
Pages 8/9: a sealion and her pup, San Salvador, Galápagos

History & *Culture*

F ew small nations can boast such ecological diversity and geographical variety, or so great a potential for natural disasters. With a Pacific coastline rich in maritime resources and a fertile coastal plain, tropical rainforest to both east and west, and the massive, earthquake-prone Andean chain studded with fertile highland valleys and sometimes menacing volcanoes in between, Ecuador has more climates than most countries ten times its size. The combination has created a nation of astounding natural beauty, and complex social and political challenges.

Early Humans

Archeology has not yet settled the vexed question of when the first humans arrived in South America, or indeed where they came from. Studies suggest they arrived about 13,000 years ago, though fresh discoveries keep pushing this date back. The prevailing theory is that they arrived in waves across the Bering Strait from Siberia, though ocean-borne migrations across the Pacific have not been ruled out.

These early hunter-gatherers found their most hospitable niche on the Pacific coast. The first permanent settlements appeared there, around 4,000BC, and South America's earliest pottery-making culture rose: the long-lived Valdivian civilization centered on the Santa Elena peninsula. These 'early Ecuadoreans' (the country was not so named until 1830) developed agriculture, growing crops such as corn and manioc, and cotton for textiles. They also became great traders, crossing the Andes and sailing along the Pacific coast.

From about 500BC onward, well-developed regional cultures flourished throughout the area that was later to become Ecuador, producing fine ceramic art almost everywhere, and exquisite gold objects at La Tolita on the north coast. In the highlands the Caras constructed huge ceremonial pyramid complexes, while the Manteño culture of the south coast developed a prosperous maritime trade.

A Clash of Empires

Around 1460, the expansion of the Inca Empire northward from Peru reached the land of the Paltas in Loja, and the Cañaris, centered at what is now the modern city of Cuenca. The Cañaris were well organized and warlike, but they were no match for the vast power of the Inca state. They succumbed, and so, one by one, did other kingdoms as the Incas drove northward. In northern Ecuador resistance stiffened, and the Incas faced a protracted campaign to subdue the Caranquis.

Left: Peruvian 18th-century painting of Atahuallpa
Right: gold earrings from La Tolita culture

All this warfare kept the Inca emperor and his armies in northern Ecuador for many years. When a mysterious and virulent epidemic, believed to be European smallpox, struck the northern Inca Empire around 1525, both Emperor Huayna Capac and his heir died, provoking a long, bloody war over the succession. Eventually, the Quito-based pretender, Atahualpa, defeated his southern rival from Cusco, Huascar, and claimed the Inca throne.

Throughout this time strange visitations had been occurring on the coast. Outlandish bearded warriors had landed from exotic wooden ships, and a small force made its way inland from northern Peru. Atahualpa committed the fatal mistake of allowing the Spaniards to proceed unimpeded into the Inca heartland, and was captured by the conquistador, Francisco Pizarro. When the Spanish killed Atahualpa native resistance splintered. Atahualpa's general Rumiñahui mounted fierce opposition in Ecuador, during which an eruption of Mt Cotopaxi drove both armies off the battlefield. Sebastián de Benalcázar finally conquered Quito and a new Spanish city rose from its ruins in 1534, followed by the port of Guayaquil, in 1535.

The early Spaniards found worlds to conquer and epic feats to accomplish. In 1541 a river expedition seeking El Dorado, led by Francisco de Orellana, was swept downstream, where it discovered and navigated the entire Amazon. The completion of the conquest left luckier conquistadors with large land-holdings in the agricultural highands, and there they settled. They lived off the toil of the Indians, most of whom sank into impoverished servitude under a system that ensured permanent indebtedness to their *patrón*. Others worked in textile sweatshops producing woolen cloth for export. The foundations of a conservative, semi-feudal society were laid. The coast was more dynamic. Cacao – the source of chocolate – became a successful cash crop, and Guayaquil thrived on trade and shipbuilding. A pattern of coast-versus-highland rivalry, which still persists, was thus set in colonial times.

The Spanish colonial regime was charged with maintaining the status quo while channeling revenues to Spain, and it did so uneventfully for nearly 300 years. The outline of a future republic first took shape in 1563, when Spain set up the Audiencia (Council) de Quito, giving some independence.

The Explorers

With its equatorial location, its towering volcanoes and its extraordinary range of natural habitats, Ecuador became a magnet for foreign explorers, naturalists, geographers and mountaineers. In 1736 a French expedition under Charles-Marie de la Condamine arrived to establish the exact location of the equator and measure the circumference of the earth. Working with Ecuadorean scholars, they took nine years to complete the task. They were followed 60 years later by Alexander von Humboldt and Aimé Bonpland. Pioneering geographers, naturalists and explorers, they roamed fruitfully across South America, making numerous scientific discoveries and amassing a vast collection of specimens. In Ecuador they attempted to climb Chimborazo, the Ecuadorean volcano then

Left: engraving of Charles Darwin, 1849

believed to be the world's highest mountain. Defeated, they nevertheless reached 5,486m (18,000ft), thought to be a human altitude record (they were unaware that the Incas had passed 6,700m/22,000ft).

In 1835 the British survey vessel HMS *Beagle* made landfall in the Galápagos and Charles Darwin spent five weeks there, making observations that would lead to one of the most earthshaking formulations of modern science: the Theory of Evolution through natural selection. Then in 1880 the British mountaineer Edward Whymper made the first ascent of Chimborazo. Scorned and disbelieved in Quito, he climbed it again. Today Ecuador is a magnet for international mountaineers.

Winds of Revolution

New ideas swept the world in the late 18th century. Enlightenment philosophers proposed new forms of government, the North Americans threw out the British, and the French threw out their king. These events electrified the *criollos* – a locally born, Spanish-descended elite – who chafed at their impotence under the narrow clericalism and excessive taxation of Spain. All positions of power were filled by men from Spain; trade or contact with any nation other than Spain was prohibited; the list of grievances was long, but the stranglehold of Madrid seemed inescapable.

Then in 1808 Napoleon invaded Spain and overthrew the monarchy, sending shockwaves throughout Spanish America. In Quito a revolutionary junta tried to seize power in 1809, but the attempt failed and the ringleaders were executed. Ten years later, however, all of South America was in revolutionary ferment. Liberating armies were converging on Ecuador from north and south. In 1820 Guayaquil declared its independence from Spain, and in 1822 Marshal Antonio Sucre, a top commander of the Venezuelan liberator Simón Bolívar, defeated the main Spanish Army at the Battle of Pichincha on the mountain slopes outside Quito, ending Spanish rule for ever.

Bolívar incorporated Ecuador into Gran Colombia, roughly covering the

Above: 1810 painting of Alexander von Humboldt and Aime Bonpland in the Tapia valley, by F.G. Weitsch

areas of modern Venezuela, Colombia and Ecuador, but the new republic lasted just seven years. In 1830 General Juan José Flores declared a new nation in the territories of the former Audiencia of Quito, naming it after the equator that ran through it. The Republic of Ecuador was born.

A Difficult Birth

General Flores and his associates ruled for 15 years, despite bitter rivalry between the old landowning oligarchy of the highlands and the merchant class of the coast. But when Flores was ousted in 1845 the country virtually disintegrated into warring regions. By 1859 Ecuador was in danger of being carved up between its more powerful neighbors, Colombia and Peru. At this critical moment an iron-willed dictator appeared on the scene: General Gabriel García Moreno, who held power until 1875.

García Moreno succeeded in uniting and defending Ecuador and modernized its infrastructure, but in many ways he was crushingly reactionary. As an ultra-conservative Catholic, he made a pact with the Vatican, letting the church levy taxes, banning other forms of religious expression, putting education in the hands of the clergy, and allowing them to censor books at will. He executed rivals and made many enemies; in 1875 he was assassinated.

More instability followed, as successive military governments struggled to balance the competing forces of coast and highlands. This period ended in the Liberal Revolution of 1895, with the ascent to power of General Eloy Alfaro. Alfaro swept away omnipresent clerical powers and established freedom of worship, civil marriage, and divorce – a radical move at that time. His government oversaw the completion of the Guayaquil-Quito railroad, begun under García Moreno – an important link in uniting the country. To this day, Alfaro's name is a rallying cry for Ecuadorean leftist movements of all stripes.

Rivalry between Eloy Alfaro and his powerful vice-president, Leonidas Plaza, eventually led to civil war. Eloy was deposed in 1911, then murdered by a Quito mob in 1912. Subsequently, a group of Guayaquil merchants known as The Ring became arbiters of all power in Ecuador, but they were overthrown in 1925, after a nosedive in world prices for cacao and a severe blight that decimated the crop. The civilian governments that followed were ineffective in the face of a gathering Great Depression, but in 1934 the

charismatic populist politician, José-María Velasco Ibarra, emerged to serve five terms as president.

War in the South

Border disputes with Peru often sputtered and flared following independence. The vaguely defined colonial borders included a vast swathe of unoccupied rainforest in the southeast, which Ecuador regarded as hers by right, but did not effectively occupy. During the late 19th and early 20th centuries, Peruvian settlers steadily entered these lands, so that by the late 1930s a *de facto* Peruvian occupation existed there. In 1941 this situation erupted into open warfare, an unequal struggle during which much of the outgunned Ecuadorean Army stayed in Quito to defend the shaky regime of President Arroyo del Río. Ecuador lost the disputed territory, and in 1942 was forced, under pressure from the United States, to sign it away via the Protocol of Rio de Janeiro. A loophole in the treaty was subsequently found, and Ecuador reaffirmed its claim, including the territory on all its national maps.

Normal relations between the two countries were stifled, and tensions erupted briefly into armed hostilities in 1981, and again, more seriously, in 1995, when a two-month battle raged over an area of mountainous forest on the Río Cenepa. Finally, in 1998, President Jamil Mahuad of Ecuador and Peruvian President Alberto Fujimori signed an agreement fixing the frontier more or less where it was in the Rio Protocol, but granting Ecuador a symbolic square kilometer, setting up contiguous national park astride the border, and allowing Ecuador navigation rights on the Peruvian Amazon.

Banana and Oil Republic

After World War II international demand catapulted Ecuador into first place as the world's largest exporter of bananas, a position it holds to this day. But the height of the boom lasted only ten years, and along with declining export revenues, Ecuador experienced a series of crisis-ridden civilian governments in the 1960s and military juntas through the 1970s. In 1964 one government did achieve important land reform, ending debt slavery, breaking up the colonial *hacienda* system and distributing land to the peasants.

In the early 1970s a new economic boom appeared over the horizon – Amazon oil – and the Oriente became the scene of a mad oil rush. Oil swiftly became the nation's biggest export earner, and Ecuador joined the oil producer's cartel, OPEC. Indigenous Amazon tribes were thrust aside, and the rainforest environment has been severely damaged in many places. Despite declining production, oil remains the major export industry, and Amazon exploration and pipeline construction continue apace.

Left: the assassination in 1921 of García Moreno, Catholic president of Ecuador
Above: 1894 illustration of an Indian man from Quito

Civilian government was restored in 1979, and has survived precariously through numerous crises and coup attempts. A decline in oil prices in the 1980s led to a huge burden of public debt, and hyper-inflation. Natural disasters added to the problem, with the 1982 El Niño devastating crops and infrastructure, and a massive earthquake in 1987 cutting off oil exports for six months.

The banana and oil prosperity reached more people than ever before, but farm workers, mainly indigenous people, were left out in the cold. The 1980s saw them mobilize under a new political umbrella movement, the CONAIE (Confederation of Indigenous Ecuadorean Nationalities). Today, though the country's native population remains on the bottom rung of the socio-economic ladder, they are a political force to be reckoned with.

After 1980, politics swung between socialist and neo-liberal reformist. In 1996 a populist former mayor of Guayaquil, Abdalá Bucaram, was elected president, but fell from grace amid clownish public antics and rampant corruption. Skyrocketing inflation and fiscal chaos led in 1997 to a general strike. Bucaram was expelled by congress, which maintained a figleaf of legality by declaring him "mentally incompetent." The following year Ecuador was again hit by El Niño, with dire economic consequences.

The 21st Century

This calamitous situation was inherited by a newly elected president, Jamil Mahuad. Faced with hyper-inflation and economic collapse, Mahuad froze US dollar bank accounts, cut fuel subsidies, increased sales tax, and defaulted on part of Ecuador's $16 billion foreign debt. Strikes and protests ensued, and in 2000, when Mahuad announced his plan to replace the almost worthless national currency with the US dollar – a move that would hit the poor hardest – *campesinos*, industrial workers, and students brought the capital to a standstill. After a failed military coup, congress once again dismissed the president, this time on the pretext that he had "abandoned his post." With consitutional order hanging by a thread, Vice-president Gustavo Noboa completed Mahuad's term of office, pressing ahead, nevertheless, with the dollarization policy. The US dollar is now the official currency of Ecuador.

Elections in 2002 brought to power a former army colonel, Lucio Gutierrez. After two years of relative calm, Gutierrez clashed with rival parties and street protesters over his dismissal of Supreme Court judges. Once again Congress ousted the president via the "abandoned his post" stratagem, and Vice-president Alfredo Palacio took charge in April 2005.

Above: Ecuadorean army soldiers and Indian protesters, January 2000

HISTORY HIGHLIGHTS

11,000BC Stone-Age hunter-gatherers appear, probably descendants of Bering Strait migrants from Siberia.

6,000BC Beginnings of rudimentary agriculture.

4,000BC First permanent settlements.

3,000BC Coastal Valdivia culture creates South America's earliest ceramics.

2,000BC Beginnings of maritime trade.

500BC–AD1480 Regional cultures flourish. La Tolita culture produces spectacular advances in metallurgy and art. Manta culture develops coastal trade.

1480–1520 Inca invasions overwhelm most regional groups.

1526 First Europeans land on the Ecuadorean coast.

1527–32 Epidemic, then civil war, weaken Inca Empire.

1532 Quito Inca Atahualpa wins war, but is captured and killed by Francisco Pizarro.

1534 Sebastián de Benalcázar defeats Incas and seizes Quito.

1541 Francisco de Orellana leads expedition which accidentally discovers and navigates the Amazon.

1563 Spain creates Audiencia (Council) de Quito, the first step toward political separation from Peru.

1687 & 1709 Guayaquil sacked by pirates.

1736 French expedition led by Charles de la Condamine determines location of equator, and measures circumference of the earth.

1802 Alexander von Humboldt and Aimé Bonpland arrive in Ecuador for scientific explorations, climb Pichincha volcano and attempt first ascent of Chimborazo.

1809 Attempt to overthrow Spanish rule fails.

1822 In the Battle of Pichincha, Liberator Marshal Sucre defeats royalist army.

1823 Simón Bolívar incorporates Ecuador into Gran Colombia.

1830 Ecuador separates and becomes independent republic.

1835 Charles Darwin spends five weeks in Galápagos, making observations that will lead to his theory of natural selection.

1852 Abolition of slavery.

1875 Assassination of conservative dictator García Moreno.

1880 Edward Whymper makes first ascent of Chimborazo.

1895 Liberal Revolution brings Eloy Alfaro to power.

1908 Completion of Guayaquil-Quito railroad.

1912 Mob kills Eloy Alfaro.

1920s Crop blight destroys vital cacao industry.

1941–2 War with Peru ends in defeat, and loss of large swathe of Amazon territory.

1947 Ecuador becomes world's largest exporter of bananas.

1964 Land reform abolishes effective serfdom and distributes land to peasantry.

1970–1980 Amazon oil pipeline construction; creates major oil industry.

1982 El Niño floods devastate coast.

1987 Massive earthquake destroys part of Trans-Andean pipeline.

1995 Border conflict with Peru.

1997 Corrupt presidency of Abdalá Bucaram ends in popular revolt and he is ousted by Congress.

1997–98 El Niño again devastates Ecuadorean economy.

1998 President Jamil Mahuad signs historic settlement of border dispute with Peru.

1999 Guagua Pichincha and Tungurahua volcanoes erupt. Quito covered in ash; Baños temporarily evacuated.

2000 President Mahuad ousted by massive protests and attempted military coup.

2002 Lucio Gutierrez, a former army colonel and organizer of the attempted coup of 2000, is elected president.

2005 Gutierrez is ousted by Congress; Vice-president Alfredo Palacio takes over the leadership.

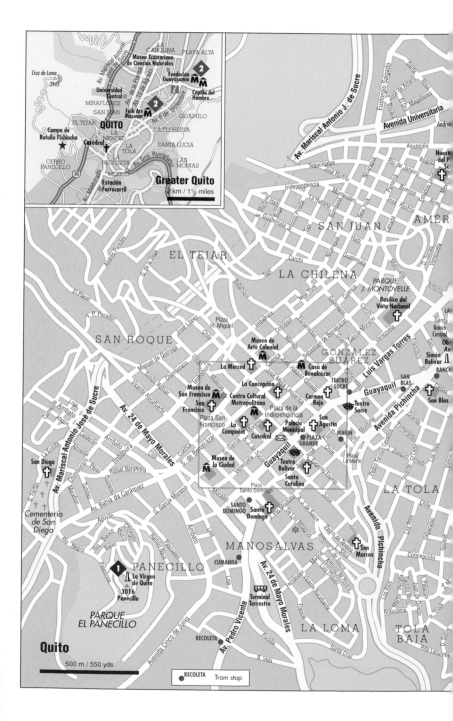

Greater Quito

2 km / 1½ miles

Quito

500 m / 550 yds

● RECOLETA Tram stop

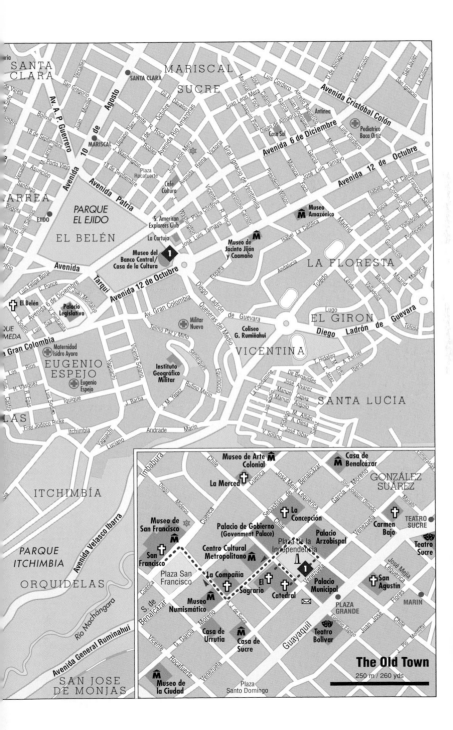

The Old Town

250 m / 260 yds

Quito & the North

Quito was settled in the first millenium AD, eventually becoming the hub of a powerful highland culture known as the Shyris. They were conquered by the Incas around 1480, and it became their northern capital for a short time, until epidemic, civil war, and Spanish conquest culminated in its destruction during a last stand here under the Inca general Rumiñawi. A Spanish city, founded in 1535, rose from the ruins, and, though partially destroyed by earthquakes since then, the old center merges colonial, republican, and modern architecture to create a unique and attractive downtown, fully worthy of the Unesco World Heritage status granted in 1979.

Quito is on a rolling plateau, oriented north–south along the eastern flanks of the mighty triple-peaked volcano, Pichincha. One of its peaks erupted violently in 1999, covering the city in ash, but the major detritus spewed westward and the city was not severely affected.

Modern Quito has a population of some 1.5 million. In the new city, the Mariscal district, just north of the main downtown park of El Ejido, is where most hotels and tourism services are located – though a major effort to spruce up the formerly run-down old city has begun to lure new hotels and services there. To the east, a valley plunges to the attractive district of Guápulo.

Most of Quito's sights are within the center, and can easily be reached by short taxi or bus rides. A new street numbering system, based on the city grid, is dysfunctional amidst the complex maze of the old city but works elsewhere. The east–west streets north of Rocafuerte, in colonial Quito, begin with N (those to the south begin with S), followed by the number of blocks, then a dash and the street number (thus N12–27 would be 12 blocks north of Rocafuerte). Likewise the north–south streets are divided between E (east) and Oe (west) at Avenida 10 de Agosto. Many buildings, especially in the old city, still bear the old street numbers.

Around Quito

The capital makes a perfect base for exploring the northern highlands, with an amazing variety of scenery and attractions close to the city: Otavalo and its famous Saturday market; subtropical Baños, with its hot springs; the cloud-forest town of Mindo; the high-altitude national park of Cotopaxi – all are less than a half-day's drive. The equatorial monument at Mitad del Mundo and the mountainous hot-springs resort of Papallacta are even closer, and a soon-to-open cable car will whisk you from La Gasca in the new city up to Cruz Loma, 4,000m (13,285ft), up on the slopes of Rucu Pichincha volcano, for a hike or just a stunning view of the city.

Left: Quito New Town, with Cayambe volcano in the distance
Right: the Virgin of Quito, from the Olga Fisch collection

1. QUITO, OLD AND NEW (see map p18–19)

Stroll among the historic churches and palaces of Quito's old center, taxi to the heights of Panecillo for terrific views of Quito, lunch at an elegant old restaurant, and return to the new town for a tour of Quito's splendid National Museum.

The old center is closed to traffic on Sundays, so this is a great day to visit. Always watch out for pickpockets, but don't be unduly paranoid – the area has been extensively renovated and is much safer than it was. Opening times of historic churches are unpredictable, but most admit visitors around 9–10am, except on Sundays, when Masses are held; you can still enter at those times, but be discreet.

Start at **Plaza de la Independencia**, the heart of old Quito, which is dominated by a huge allegorical monument to independence. When starting late, a good way to get an overview of the center is to take a ride in one of the horse-drawn carriages (Mon–Fri 4pm–11pm, Sat 11am–midnight, Sun 11am–10pm) that start from the north-east corner of the square .

Otherwise, begin with a visit to the **Catedral** (Mon–Fri 10am–4pm, Sat 10am–2pm), an opulent building occupying an entire side of the square, which shelters the remains of the great independence hero, Marshall Sucre. Its construction was begun around 1550, making it one of the earliest cathedrals of South America. There are some superb religious paintings of the Quito school – painted by Spanish-trained Indian artists who were often anonymous. Attached to the cathedral on the west side of the building stands the chapel of **El Sagrario**, a very beautiful example of baroque *mestizo* (mixed indigenous/European culture) architecture.

The columns and arches of the **Palacio de Gobierno** (Government Palace) fill the west side of the square. You can lean past the lance-toting ceremonial guards to glimpse, through the imposing doorway, a mosaic mural of Francisco de Orellana's navigation of the Amazon, by Ecuador's most famous modern artist, Oswaldo Guayasamín. Make your way south along Calle García Moreno. The next corner features the **Centro Cultural Metropolitano**, an old building, formerly a Spanish military headquarters, where the revolutionary heroes of 1809 were held, then executed (a small waxworks exhibit depicts this part of its history); it is now reborn as a modern exhibition hall with temporary exhibits that are open to the public free of charge.

At the end of the block is **La Compañía**, the renowned Jesuit church whose elaborate baroque *mestizo* stone facade is a classic of the distinctive high Jesuit style of early colonial times. The church is undergoing extended restorations, but it is usually possible to visit. Its graphic painting of hell has terrified thousands of sinners since the 17th century. The walls, vaults,

Above: Plaza Independencia   **Above Right:** fine old doorway
Right: mass being celebrated in San Francisco church

and cupola display staggering amounts of gold-leaf – supposedly, 7 tons of it.

Turn right on Sucre and emerge onto the broad expanse of **Plaza San Francisco**. Often there are street musicians and performers, and it's a great place to people-watch and chat with strolling *Quiteños*. Stop at Tianguez, the outdoor café and restaurant right on the square's northwest corner, for good coffee, a terrific fruit juice, and a delicious *empanada,* the local pastry snack.

San Francisco, Quito's largest church, looms on a terrace high above the west edge of the square. Behind its austere facade lies a vast and opulent space filled with splendid colonial art, including an Assumption of the Virgin by the famous Indian painter, Caspicara, and a magnificent altarpiece, incorporating a winged virgin carved by Bernardo de Legarda, which served as the prototype for the enormous Virgin of Quito on the Panecillo. Earthquakes destroyed the original *mudéjar* (Moorish-influenced) architecture of the nave, but this can still be seen within the dome. The adjacent museum, the **Museo de San Francisco** (Mon–Sat 9am–1pm & 2pm–6pm, Sun 9am–noon), is worth visiting for its extensive collection of religious art, with an allegorical series by Miguel de Santiago, a crucifixion with some of the most anatomically excruciating wounds you will see outside of an emergency room, and many works by some of the most famous Quito artists of colonial times.

The **Panecillo** (little breadloaf) is a hill rising abruptly to the south of the old city, crowned by a massive 41-m (135-ft) statue of **La Virgin de Quito**. It is not considered safe to go there on foot. Take a taxi and keep it with you for your return journey. The unusual image of a winged Virgin trampling a chained serpent (symbolizing her power to overcome sin and ascend to heaven) was conceived as a dedication of all Ecuador to the

Virgin, during a time of strong clerical influence, and completed almost 100 years later, in 1975. You can climb the hollow interior for a superb panoramic view of Quito and, on a clear day, the surrounding volcanoes. On the slopes to the west a monument marks the spot where Sucre defeated Spanish forces in 1822.

Return to Plaza Independencia for lunch amidst the muted and traditional ambience of the Cueva del Oso ($$), Chile 1046 y Venezuela, tel: 257-2786. The seafood is recommended. Half a block up on the same side of the square, a food hall in the Palacio Arzobispal has a variety of inexpensive restaurants.

The National Museum

From the Plaza, take a taxi, or for a more local experience, stroll three blocks down Avenida Chile to La Marín, the terminus for the Ecovía bus line, and take the first bus heading out. You'll drive past **Parque La Alameda**, the site of South America's oldest astronomical observatory, and then Parque El Ejido, before alighting at the Casa de Cultura bus stop, for a visit to the **Museo del Banco Central de la Reserva** (Tues–Fri 9am–5pm), Ecuador's national museum. It would be easy to spend a whole afternoon browsing around this varied and fascinating collection, and English-speaking guides are available by appointment (tel: 222-3258). The archeology gallery is for most

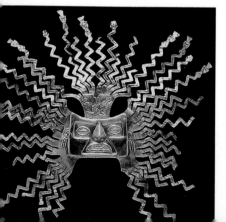

people the star of the show, with a big collection of exquisite ceramics and stone objects from as early as 4,000BC. The gold room is a highlight here, showing the evolution of metallurgy, culminating in a famous gold headdress from the Tolita culture. Other galleries display Ecuador's art across the centuries; there's plenty from the colonial era, and the republican and contemporary galleries have works by Ecuador's best-known modern artists.

Above: view from Panecillo
Left: Pre-Columbian gold sun mask

2. GUAYASAMIN MUSEUMS *(see map p18–19)*

These two galleries feature the wrenching work of the late Oswaldo Guayasamín, the most prominent and internationally acclaimed of Ecuador's many accomplished artists. The Olga Fisch Museum of Folk Art offers a soothing contrast.

To see both museums the same day (and benefit from a price reduction for a combined ticket), go between Tuesday and Friday. From the Mariscal, take a taxi or board the Ecovía northbound on 6 de Diciembre. Get off at Ignacio Bossano, walk north one long block on 6 de Diciembre and turn right up the hill on Bosmediano for a stiff climb to the Fundación – and then uphill again, going right on Carbo then left on Calvache, to the Capilla del Hombre.

Born in Quito in 1919 of an Indian father and *mestizo* mother, Oswaldo Guayasamín's life and work spanned most of the 20th century, which he regarded as 'the worst century that men have lived on earth'. His art is not everyone's cup of tea. He chose to express the pain and suffering he saw in life, and especially in the lives of the indigenous Ecuadorean poor. Even his land- and cityscapes seem to run with blood or simmer with lurking dread. Some of his work was angrily and explicitly political – *Meeting at the Pentagon*, a well-known painting, is virtually a political cartoon – yet there is no denying his talent, or the force and originality of his work. He is considered the greatest modern artist Ecuador has produced.

Guayasamín himself set up the two museums featuring his work, and both are located in the Bellavista area of the new town. The **Fundación Guayasamín** (Bosmediano, E15–68, tel: 244-6455; Mon–Fri 10am–5pm) is the smaller of the two, in an intimate garden setting. It also displays the artist's collection of pre-hispanic and colonial art. **La Capilla del Hombre** (Mariano Calvache y Lorenzo Chavez, tel: 244-8492; Tues–Sun 10am–5pm; admission charge), on which Guayasamín was working when he died in 1999, is rather more grandiose, emanating, perhaps, from just a hint of megalomania.

Folklore Museum

It's well worth allowing enough time to see something completely different. Take the Ecovía back along 6 de Diciembre, get off at Colón, and climb uphill on that street to visit the **Folk Art Museum** (Colón E10-53 y Caamaño, Mon–Fri 9am–7pm, Sat 9am–1pm & 3–7pm; tel: 254-1315; free), which was set up by the late Olga Fisch on the premises of her store, Folklore. The collection is small but superb, as you would expect from a woman who devoted her life to, and became the godmother and promoter of Ecuadorean handicrafts. If it's lunch or dinnertime by now, you can combine this visit with a fancy meal of excellent Ecuadorean cuisine, surrounded by more folk art, at El Galpón (tel: 254-6961), which is around the back at the same address.

Right: sculpture by Oswaldo Guayasamín

3. Mitad del Mundo and Pululahua
(see map p27)

The equator, which gives the country its name, has inspired a monument just north of Quito. Unexpectedly, you will find not one, but two equators marked out, along with a complex of museums. Nearby, an ancient volcano offers views over the rim and a pleasant hike down into the crater.

On weekends there is free live music and entertainment, but it's very crowded on Sundays, so Saturday is probably the best day. Leave Quito by about 9am, taking a taxi (half-hour drive, about $15) or a northbound 'Mitad del Mundo' bus on Avenida América north of Avenida Pérez Guerrero.

In 1736 Charles-Marie de la Condamine and his French and Ecuadorean cohorts began nine years of studies in Ecuador, to establish the location of the equator and measure the circumference of the earth. Today a monument and the Mitad del Mundo visitor complex commemorates this effort and marks the equatorial line. Though unashamedly touristy, it's pleasant and entertaining, and is well worth a visit.

To Pululahua

To make a full day of this excursion, incorporating some hiking and fresh air, include a visit to nearby **Pululahua** (Poo-loo-la-wa), a massive dormant volcano, and hike down into the floor of the crater. It's important to go in the morning, because the area is often cloudy later on. When the bus from Quito deposits you at the traffic circle in front of Mitad del Mundo, ignore this complex for the time being and hop on any bus marked "Calacali" for a journey of 2km (1¼ miles). Get off the bus at the right-hand turning to El Crater Restaurant and take the ten-minute walk there.

From here there is a splendid view down into the crater, with its farmland floor and wooded slopes. The entire area is a geo-botanical reserve, noted for orchids and butterflies. You can descend to the bottom via a footpath passing through varying ecological zones, and the round trip takes about two hours. The crater is fairly dry in this eastern portion, but to the west it slopes off into the lush Pacific region climate. For an excellent (expensive) lunch, El Crater (tel: 243-9254, www.elcrater.com), part of a new and rather upscale hotel ($$$$ – *see page 79 for price guide*) and spa, has a terrific view over the rim. If the idea of exploring one of the world's only inhabited volcanic craters appeals, the Green Horse Ranch (tel: 237-4847, www.horseranch.de), located inside the crater, offers horseback excursions.

Above: tourists straddle the equatorial line at Mitad del Mundo

Zero Degrees Latitude

Return to **Mitad del Mundo** (Mon–Thur 9am–6pm, Fri–Sun 9am–7pm). The **Equator Monument** (admission charge) is always swarming with people having their photo taken with one foot in each hemisphere. Unfortunately, la Condamine's measurement, where this line was drawn, was 240m (787ft) south of the true equator (*see below*), but Mitad del Mundo has plenty of attractions of its own. The monument houses an interesting ethnographic museum; from the top, which has a sweeping view, you descend through a series of displays of Ecuador's many ethnic groups and sub-cultures.

To one side of the monument there is a village modeled on a colonial settlement, with handicraft stores, restaurants, and a post office (mail postcards here for an "Equator" postmark). Opposite is a row of small museums, one with a model of Quito, and a planetarium (Tues–Sun 9am–4pm; admission charge). The **Solar Culture Museum** (free) exhibits the models and theories of the Ecuadorean archeologist Cristobal Cobo, who claims that indigenous people determined the location of the equator as early AD1100, and did it far more precisely than La Condamine: on the nearby Catequilla hill, an ancient platform at exactly 0° 0' 0" lies at the center of a complex web of far-flung ancient sites, all linked by solstice/equinox, sunrise/sunset points.

To add confusion, there seems to be another equator – some claim it to be the real one – 200m (656ft) north, outside the main gates of Mitad del Mundo (bring your GPS device to be certain) at the **Inti Ñan Museum** (daily 9am–6pm; admission charge). This funky, somewhat eclectic museum features weaving displays, mock-ups of indigenous dwellings, and demonstrations of equatorial precision. Here you can actually witness water going straight down a drain without producing a vortex and see an egg balancing on the head of a nail, both phenomena allegedly proving the absence of the Coriolis force at this point. Bad science, perhaps, but hugely entertaining.

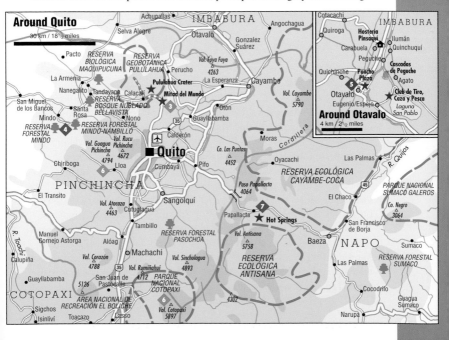

4. MINDO AND THE TANDAYAPA VALLEY
(see map p27)

A two- to four-day excursion west across the coastal range, two hours by road from Quito, where a tropical area of lush cloudforest valleys, mountain streams, and waterfalls has become a popular destination for outdoor and eco-tourism activities.

Not recommended in January and February, due to heavy rains and swollen rivers. Take swimwear, insect repellent, raingear, flashlight, and binoculars. Mindo gets packed on weekends, so weekdays are best. From Quito take the Flor del Valle bus, whose terminal is at Manuel Larrea y Asunción (tel: 252-7495) – it's safer and more convenient than the Terminal Terrestre. Departures are at 8am and 3.45pm, plus 7am and 9am on weekends. Make advance reservations for the Bellavista Reserve if you plan to include it in the trip.

Abrupt geographical contrasts within short distances are a constant feature of travel in Ecuador, but they seldom get more abrupt than this. The coast road northwest to Esmeraldas winds from the well-watered Quito plateau across a dry landscape around Mitad del Mundo and Calacalí, then plunges through steep gorges clad in dense forest on a highway lined with orchids, crossing the Tandayapa and Mindo valleys. An alternative route on the old road through Nono is more tranquil, with superb scenery and excellent bird-watching on the western slope. A bumpy route with little traffic (the only transportation is a rather expensive rental car or taxi), it has been designated Ecuador's first 'eco-route,' though its future effect on the area is unclear.

An Ecological Wonderland
The belt of highland forest known as the **Chocó**, which extends north from here into Colombia, is considered one of the world's biodiversity hotspots. More than 350 bird species have been logged in the Mindo/Tandayapa area,

Above: waterfall at the Bellavista Cloud Forest Reserve

and the combination of steep terrain and frequent rainfall has created the scores of dramatic waterfalls that are part of the area's great attractions. In much of coastal Ecuador the forest has been slashed and burned away, but here local efforts have preserved extensive swathes of native vegetation. The **Reserva Forestal Mindo-Nambillo** protects 192sq. km (74sq. miles) of varied habitats across an altitude range from 1,200–4,200m (3,935–13,775ft). Private reserves abutting this zone, effectively increase its size. The laying of an oil pipeline through here in 2002 left its mark, but has so far failed to accelerate the destruction of the area, as many had feared.

Three blocks from the main street is the Cabañas Armonía (tel: 276-5471, www.orchids-birding.com; $$; *see page 92 for price guide*), owned by Hugolino Oñate, an orchid enthusiast and birding guide (Spanish-speaking only). The cabins are set in the midst of an exotic orchid garden. One unusual and interesting birdwatching option here is to visit a 'lek' – a sort of avian singles bar – where numerous colorful and raucous male Cocks-of-the-Rock display and compete for a mate.

For more upscale accommodations try El Monte (tel: 276-5427; www.ecuadorcloudforest.com; $$$$, includes all meals), about 3km (2 miles) outside the town, which has a private reserve with tours, its own waterfall, and very comfortable lodges. The resort will arrange pick-up and transfer from their café in Mindo. For eating in Mindo, El Chef restaurant and Mindo Café are recommended for local food, and the El Rincón del Rio for pizza. The Mindo area has various fish farms, so fresh trout and tilapia are always on somebody's menu.

A popular diversion here is innertubing, known as *regatas*, which is like a boisterous aquatic theme-park ride. It's an inexpensive and fun way to spend a couple of hours getting to know the rapids of the Río Mindo. Hotels and several agencies in town offer this sport. Just out of town the Motmot Inn (tel: 257-2851) is recommended. By taking the morning bus from Quito you can do this activity in the afternoon. The tourist information office (erratic opening hours) on the corner of Mindo's main square, has information about other options, such as horseback riding and mountain biking.

Butterflies and Waterfalls

The **Mindo Butterfly Farm** (daily 9am–3pm) is an unusual and rewarding way to start the next day. Follow it with a few hours of forest walking and swimming in the Nambillo waterfalls area. Bring water and a packed lunch for this excursion. Take a pick-up to the Butterfly Farm, about 3km (2 miles) southeast of Mindo, and have it wait for you. The butterfly farm staff (English spoken) will introduce you to their breeding program and the life cycle of the butterfly, including a fascinating display of jewel-like tropical chrysalids.

Right: lush vegetation at Bellavista Cloud Forest Reserve

Then you are free to wander in the netted compound where brilliant turquoise morphos, swallowtails, and many other species flutter in profusion.

Take the taxi back towards Mindo, cross the bridge, and drive upstream to the trailhead at the **Nambillo waterfalls area** (admission charge). Arrange for the taxi driver to pick you up later, or be prepared to walk the 6km (4 miles) back into Mindo. Near the trailhead a low-tech cable car known as a *tarabita* (fee) swings visitors across a wooded ravine. From here a network of marked trails leads to different spots: the well-known Nambillo Falls, a 15-minute walk, with an optional 10-m (33-ft) leap into the pool for daredevil visitors; a series of five smaller falls downhill from the *tarabita*,

strung along a lesser tributary of the Nambillo; and, about 1 hour's walk upvalley, the recently opened Reina cascade, a bigger but less-visited waterfall. The forest is good for birdwatching and orchid-spotting. You can choose whichever spot pleases you for lunch and swimming, and either walk or take the *tarabita* back to the trailhead.

A Cloud Forest Sojourn

You can extend your visit to take in a more isolated, pristine cloudforest zone at higher altitude by spending a night or two at the **Bellavista Cloud Forest Reserve** (tel: 223-2313 from Quito; www.bellavistacloudforest.com; $$$$). Reservations are essential here, since they often receive groups and there are no alternative lodgings in the vicinity. The lodge has shared accommodations or the option of camping.

Leaving Mindo, take local transportation or a pick-up to the main highway, wait there and flag down any bus heading for Quito. Get off at Nanegalito, about 20km (12 miles) along the highway, and hire a pick-up (about $15) to take you up the narrow dirt road to Bellavista.

The lodge stands in a 700-hectare (1,730-acre) private reserve, and was built by Anglo-Colombian couple, Richard Parsons and Gloria Nicholls. The main building is an unusual geodesic wood dome, with a creaky spiral stairway up the middle, and a circular veranda swarming with hummingbirds, lured by the many feeders – it has an altogether eccentric and amiable atmosphere in an amazingly peaceful location.

Without much effort you will see dozens of bird species here, some very colorful. The place is popular with hard-core birders, but equally suitable for those more generally interested in the wilderness experience. English-speaking trail and birding guides are available. There are 10km (6 miles) of steep forest trails – including a self-guided one with didactic information boards – three waterfalls, and a bewildering variety of vegetation. Make arrangements with the lodge for your return to the highway and Quito.

Above: the main lodge at Bellavista Cloud Forest Reserve

5. OTAVALO *(see map p27)*

Head for the highlands to visit the famous market in Otavalo, spend the night at a colonial-style *hacienda* and shop for excellent leather goods at Cotacachi.

Saturday – market day – is the best time to visit Otavalo, but there is some market action every day except Sunday. From Quito, take the fast and inexpensive ($7.50 per person) Supertaxis Los Lagos (Asunción 3–82, tel: 256-5992) – organize this by phone (two days in advance if traveling Fri or Sat); they will pick you up anywhere in the new city. Otavalo-bound buses can be caught on Avenida Occidental in the new city. Ibarra- and Tulcán-bound buses also work, but only if traveling light and arriving at Otavalo in daylight, since they drop you on the highway, quite far from the center.

Otavalan Culture

Otavalo is the hub of a highland region and an indigenous ethnic group that has maintained its cultural continuity for many centuries. Their appearance is distinctive. Men wear their hair in a long braid (though young men now wear ponytails), usually topped with a felt hat, and sport a poncho and baggy calf-length white pants. Women's dress is as close to the clothing of imperial Inca times as anything you will see in the Andes today: a split skirt (worn with a modest underskirt since the missionaries arrived), and a folded cloth on their heads. Their throats are adorned with copious and costly gold necklace, status symbols that are actually Christmas-tree ornaments imported from the Czech Republic.

Known as the Caras in ancient times, the Otavaleños distinguished themselves by fighing off the Incas for 17 years before finally succumbing. They acquired the Inca language, still widely spoken as the Quichua dialect, but long before the Incas, Ecuador had developed a

Above: the market in Otavalo
Right: young Otavalo girl and baby

trans-Andean and coastal trading system and an itinerant merchant class who traveled the trade routes. The Otavaleños are hardy survivors and upholders of this tradition. You may occasionally spot them on the streets of major cities in Europe or the Americas, playing their music or peddling handicrafts. Almost alone among Andean natives, Otavaleños have managed to both prosper within the modern cash economy and maintain their ethnic identity.

The Saturday Market

Today the Saturday market attracts flocks of tourists, but those who accuse it of being touristy are rather missing the point – selling to outsiders has always been the business of this town. And if you want to get away from fellow tourists, you just have to leave the main Plaza de Ponchos and within a block or two you are in among the local people's markets.

Though you can leave Quito early on Saturday and get to Otavalo in plenty of time for the market, even making it a day trip, it's more relaxing to arrive on Friday night. There are several old *haciendas* here, including the famous Hacienda Cusín and the more economical Casa de Hacienda. If you prefer a spacious central hotel, the Ali Shungu *(see page 93)* is hard to beat.

Early risers wanting to enjoy an experience definitely not aimed at tourists should go to the Saturday morning livestock market. Here you can observe the local bargaining system at work – it starts at sunrise and finishes by about 9am. Walk west on Calle Colón from the town center, cross the Pan-American highway and it's just beyond the sports stadium.

The **Plaza de Ponchos** is a sumptuous shopping feast of densely packed handicraft stalls (beware of pickpockets). Otavaleños not only weave and produce craft items themselves, they also import artisan goods from throughout the Andean countries. Quality is generally good, but variable (for the very best you should shop at one of the high-end craft shops in Quito), and polite bargaining is acceptable. Embroidered cotton garments, woven wool blankets, ponchos and wall hangings, sweaters, hats, bags, jewelry, and pottery are just a few of the items for sale here. *Shigras* – once-ubiquitous colorful

Above: view of Cotacachi mountain, near Otavalo

bags woven from sisal – have been driven close to extinction by cheap plastic alternatives, but can still be found. If the crowds get too much for you, retire to the second-floor Buena Vista Café on Calle Salinas, overlooking the square, for good espresso or fruit juice and a superb view of the market.

Leaving the crafts behind, take a stroll four blocks along Calle Jaramillo up to the old food market area, starting at Calle Montalvo. An incredible variety of Ecuadorean produce is on sale, and a real insight on local life. Have lunch with live Andean music at the Ali Shungu restaurant (tel: 292-0750) at the corner of Calle Quito and Egas. It has an outdoor garden terrace and delicious fresh food, mostly vegetarian but with some excellent meat dishes, and such exotica as trout enchiladas.

Cotacachi and Some Weavers' Workshops

If you are still in shopping mode, and leather goods interest you, walk or take a taxi to the bus station (about 12 blocks), and take a pleasant 20-minute bus ride through rolling farmland to Cotacachi. Very clean and visitor-friendly, this town specializes in leather – riding saddles, coats and jackets, purses, luggage, wallets – with many stores on the main street, and they will bargain.

An alternative, more outdoorsy excursion – also with shopping possibilities – takes you through small villages around Otavalo to visit local weavers. This can be done on foot or by taxi, but the most efficient and agreeable way is to rent a bicycle from Ali Shungu or Jatun Pacha *(see Accommodations listings).* Don't leave the bike unattended. Take the Pan-American highway north for about 1.5km (1 mile) and take the right-hand turn-off to

the village of **Peguche**, where weaver José Cotachachi and family have a gallery just to the right of the church. From here you can head south on a dirt road, returning via the **Cascada de Peguche**, a pretty waterfall. Head west (right) from the waterfall to Otavalo.

For a longer excursion, go north from Peguche through Quinchuqui and then south toward Lago San Pablo. At the village of **Agato** visit Tahantinsuyu, the worskshop of the Andrango family, famous weavers who give demonstrations and sell their work. Continue south from Agato to meet the main highway that circles the lake. Turn right and flag down a bus, or cycle back to Otavalo, turning right again when you meet the Pan-American highway.

If you stay another day in the Otavalo area, there's a beautiful hike around **Cuicocha**, a limpid blue lake at the foot of 4,939-m (16,216-ft) **Cotacachi volcano**. It takes about 5 hours, plus time to get there and back. (Robberies have occurred here, so do not carry valuables and walk with a group if possible.) There is no public transportation. Hire a taxi to take you from Cotacachi, and arrange to be picked up later. To avoid getting stranded, do not pay until the end – it's an additional 3-hour walk back to Cotacachi.

Right: carving of the crucifixion at the Hacienda Cusin, Lago San Pablo

6. AVENUE OF VOLCANOES
AND COTOPAXI *(see map p27)*I

Heading south between Quito and Latacunga the Pan-American highway follows a valley of lush farmland flanked on either side by a dozen volcanoes, three of them with permanent snow. The greatest of them is Cotopaxi, the centerpiece of one of Ecuador's best-known national parks.

Make reservations for accommodations and transportation, and if you want to climb Cotopaxi, arrange for a professional guide. The best months to do the climb are December through February, when there is less cloud; June through August is even clearer, but very windy.

To avoid crowds, avoid weekends. Take a sleeping bag for the climber's refuge, high-factor sunblock, warm hiking socks, and quality sport long underwear (not cotton), plus your own basic equipment for the lesser hikes. Bring toilet paper and a padlock for the lockers at the climber's refuge. The outfitters supply everything else. Currently, the entry fee for the national park is $10, and the refuge costs $12.50 per night (cash only).

Even in a nation of highly active volcanoes, Cotopaxi stands out for its recent history of massive and destructive eruptions, one of which, in 1534, supposedly drove warring Spaniards and Incas off the battlefield. Later the mountain resumed violent activity for long periods through the 18th and 19th centuries. It was fairly quiet through the 20th century, and remains so, though its subterranean rumblings must be constantly monitored.

Altitude Acclimatization

One exciting possibility in Ecuador is to scale this imposing peak without undue risk. Despite being Ecuador's second-highest peak (5,897m/19,637ft), **Cotopaxi** is considered a beginner's climb; any reasonably fit individual with some altitude hiking experience can reach the summit. It's essential, though, that you undertake a period of altitude acclimatization before attempting this, including a couple of non-technical climbs of lower peaks. The best plan is to do acclimatization hikes and climb at the end of a stay in highland Ecuador, not immediately on arrival. If possible, schedule your climb for around full moon; not only is the weather said to be best then, but since ascents begin around 1am, moonlight is both useful and enchanting.

The possibilities for acclimatization climbs are almost infinite. The imminent opening of the **Teleferico** to Cruz Loma in Quito will make it easy to summit **Rucu Pichincha** (4,672m/15,112ft) from Quito, a gratifying outdoor experience in itself, with superb views of the city. (Currently Rucu Pichincha has serious crime problems, but since the Teleferico is a major recreation area development, security will presumably be improved. Check with South American Explorers *(see page 98)* for the latest situation.) From Cruz Loma

Above: local cowhands near Cotopaxi National Park
Right: Cotopaxi, with Tambopaxi hostel in the foreground

beginners should take the right-hand trail that traverses below the cliffs, then ascends easier slopes to the summit; more experienced climbers can take the direct route up the summit ridge. You may also consider a hike up the nearby peak of **Guagua Pichincha** (4,794m/15,660ft); an easy climb, but it requires transportation beyond the village of Lloa. Consider signing up for a tour, or finding companions and hiring a pick-up. By acclimatizing with hikes out of Quito, it is indeed possible to spend one night at the climber's refuge, climb Cotopaxi, and return to Quito the following evening. However, that way you miss the entire experience of Cotopaxi National Park and the surrounding countryside.

To see **Cotopaxi National Park** and enjoy a couple of great acclimatization hikes on the mountain heights, take four nights out of Quito, summiting Cotopaxi on the last morning. As an alternative, some agencies offer mountain-biking trips in the park *(see Useful Addresses, page 98)*.

Spend three nights at Tambopaxi Acclimatization Center (tel: 222-0242 in Quito; www.tambopaxi.com; $$$ full board), located within the park near the foot of Cotopaxi. The center is hostel-style, with dormitories, bunk beds, and shared bathrooms, but it's very comfortable and friendly, with good food (or bring a tent and camp; small fee includes use of showers). On hiking days, ask for a packed lunch or bring your own trail food with you.

Climbing Cotopaxi

The final night is spent at the climber's refuge. Two recommended outfitters for the Cotopaxi ascent are: Compañía de Guías de Alta Montaña (Jorge Washington 425 y 6 de Diciembre, tel: 290-1551; www.compania deguias.com), and Safari Tours *(see page 98)*. Both offer skilled and experienced service, plus clothing and equipment for the climb. The latter is less expensive, with slightly older but still serviceable gear.

Make travel arrangements with Tambopaxi *(see above)*, or, if going all the way by bus then on foot, leave Quito by 9.30am (timing is important). Carry water, and food for lunch. Ideally take either the Mejía or the Brito bus line, which go into Machachi itself. Otherwise, take any bus heading toward Latacunga and points south, and get off at the Machachi turn-off, about 40 minutes from Quito. From there it's a short walk to the left into the town

center. An easy option is to then hire a pick-up in the square, which will take you to Tambopaxi for about $20–25. Otherwise take the Dolorosa bus for El Pedregal (6.30am and 11.30am; confirm times with Tambopaxi) from outside the church in Machachi. Get off the bus at Santa Ana de Pedregal, before the final stop, and start hiking southeast along the dirt road signposted to Porvenir. This is a beautiful walk of about 9km (5 miles), across the high plateau, finishing at 3,750m (12,300ft). Carrying a backpack, this takes in the region of 3–4 hours.

Tambopaxi is well placed for ascents of **Rumiñahui** and **Sincholagua**, and the staff can help you find the routes. Start early for both these climbs. They are moderate, with a bit of scrambling at the top, but be aware that bad weather and especially electric storms make any mountain dangerous; if in doubt, turn back. The rolling *páramo* grassland of the national park is an austere and treeless yet beautiful environment, so hiking here is much more than a mere workout. Birds are plentiful, especially in wetland areas, and you may see Andean condors soaring around the peaks. The culpeo fox is commonly seen, especially in the early morning, as are its prey, rabbits. Wild horses also roam the area.

Rumiñahui is the easiest and should be attempted the first day; its central peak (4,712m/15,190ft) is the best one. Climb Sincholagua (4,893m/15,985ft) the following day; arrange with Tambopaxi for transportation to the trailhead, and return on foot. The mountain has some tough going on scree and the final few meters are slightly alarming. Rather than exhaust yourself here, you might want to save energy for the following day

The Big One

Next day your guide should pick you up mid-morning for the drive to the car park and a 40-minute haul with all your gear to the refuge at 4,800m (15,745ft). Use a locker and watch your gear here. You'll get a bit of cram-

pon practice on a nearby glacier tongue. Stow batteries in a warm pocket, so they won't fail in freezing temperatures. After dinner you rest, then breakfast around midnight before setting off for the summit – standard practice so you can descend before the sun turns the snow into a sticky mess and raises avalanche danger. It should take 5–8 hours for the climb (2–3 hours for the descent) and you should be more than halfway up as dawn approaches. This can be breathtaking in clear weather, as the sun lights up the volcanoes and numerous lesser peaks. To stand on Cotopaxi's mighty rim looking down into the crater's steaming vents is a moment of great personal triumph for a first-time mountaineer.

Left: nearing the summit of Cotopaxi

quito & the north

7. HOT SPRINGS & HIGHLANDS: PAPALLACTA
(see map p27)

A one-day or overnight trip east of Quito, where an abundant hot-springs source has been turned into a charming complex of outdoor baths and swimming pools, with a volcano dominating the skyline.

Try to visit Papallacta during the week, because weekends get very busy. Bring swimming gear. There are frequent buses (1½ hours) from the Terminal Terrestre in Quito (Baeza or Tena routes, but not Tena via Baños). There's a 1.5-km (1-mile) walk or taxi ride at the other end (see below), or you can organize transportation through your hotel.

Ecuador has many hot-springs resorts. **Papallacta** has the advantage of being close to Quito, beautifully designed, well maintained and in a scenic woodland setting, with a rushing mountain stream close by. The resort is 3,300m (10,890ft) up on the edge of the Cayambe-Coca ecological reserve, which stretches north along the Andes, and you can take a walk on a self-guided trail through high-altitude forest filled with hummingbirds. Snowcapped Antisana (5,758m/18,860ft) is one of the spectacular volcanoes on the skyline.

A day visit to Papallacta can be very economical, and there is a good, reasonably priced restaurant right by the pools. For an overnight stay, the luxurious Termas Hotel (tel: 256-8989; www.termaspapallacta.com; $$$), has its own private pools and a health spa, or there's the more modest Hostería La Pampa (tel: 248-6286; $$) near the turn-off to the main road.

The journey from Quito crosses a high pass through beautiful *páramo* (high Andean grassland) and descends into the fringes of the Amazon basin. Currently, the turn-off to the springs is on the main highway, and is about 1.5km (1 mile) from the springs, but a new paved highway route beginning about 4km (3 miles) before the hot springs turn-off is under construction, and when completed will take the main road farther away. New arrangements for getting from the highway to the springs may be operating by the time you read this. To return to Quito, just flag down one of the frequent buses on the highway – but do this during daylight hours.

Above: the public baths in the hot springs at Papallacta

The Central & Southern Highlands

From Quito the green central valleys of highland Ecuador roll southward, one after the other, seated at a comfortable altitude between the western and eastern ranges of the Andes. Passing within sight of most of Ecuador's major snow-capped volcanoes, the route south from Quito is also the major arterial highway of the highlands, serving a chain of medium-sized provincial capitals and country market towns.

West of Latacunga lies a region of rolling pastureland cleft by ravines and small canyons where rivers have cut deep into the soft volcanic ash that built these hills. Though the area lacks the drama of a lofty snow-peaked volcano, the flooded but potentially active crater of Quilotoa, with its sulfurous turquoise lake, offers plenty of visual excitement and awesome imaginings of the titanic upheavals that created this bucolic countryside.

East of Ambato the Río Pastaza cuts down between two remote and mountainous areas now designated as Llanganates and Sangay national parks, forming broad a valley that becomes increasingly lush but also narrower as you head east toward the Amazon basin. Here lies the resort town of Baños, with copious hot springs, captivating waterfalls, and hiking areas that have made this town a favorite destination for national tourists.

South of Ambato, Riobamba is the starting point for a short journey on a small remaining piece of what was once known as 'the world's most difficult railroad.' Started in the 1870s, the track from Guayaquil to Quito kept advancing through civil wars, revolutions, and volcanic eruptions, finally reaching Quito in 1908. The very emblem of Ecuador's march toward modernity through most of the 20th century, most of it was ultimately shut down by natural disasters and modern roadbuilding. This section, built over a vertical cliff known as the Devil's Nose, is a piece of living history.

Farther south the volcanoes are left behind, giving way to older mountains and the provinces of Cañar and Azuay. Here you will find Ecuador's best-preserved Inca ruins at Ingapirca, where they dominate a highland landscape on the former royal Inca highway from Cusco to Quito.

Cuenca, center of a broad valley where four rivers converge, was once the stronghold of the Cañari Indians, still numerous in the region today. The Incas conquered them and renamed their city Tomebamba, only to be conquered themselves by the Spanish conquistadors, who founded the city of Cuenca on the Inca ruins. Ecuador's third-largest city, Cuenca is a conservative place that maintains its heritage, a place that is considered a jewel of New World Spanish architecture. It was designated a Unesco World Heritage Site in 1999.

Left: Tungurahua erupts
Right: Inca mortar and pestle at Ingapirca

8. MARKET VILLAGES AND QUILOTOA CRATER
(see map p44)

Take two nights out of Quito to visit a peaceful area off the beaten track, taking in the beautiful flooded volcano of Quilotoa, and exploring one of the area's many markets.

It's worth planning to visit on a Thursday to catch the main market, but there are others on Sunday and Monday. Take any bus from Quito to Lata-cunga or points south (frequent departures; journey about 2 hours), timing your arrival to connect with the Vivero bus to Isinliví, which leaves from the main bus terminal at 1pm every day except Thursday, when it leaves from Saquisilí at 11am. The journey to Isinliví takes about 3 hours.

The dairy and wool farmers of the region around Quilotoa frequently converge on the scattered village markets that take place throughout the week, crowned by the mother of them all – the Thursday market at **Saquisilí**. This market is huge, varied, busy, untouristy, and quite fascinating. If you visit the area and plan to return through Zumbahua early on a Thursday morning, you can make a small detour to visit Saquisilí market on your way back to Quito. To experience a quieter rural market, extend this trip and visit Gauntualo, near Isinliví (Mon), Chugchilán or Sigchos (Sun) or Zumbahua (Sat).

The area is far from overrun with tourists, but a few small inns have opened north of Quilotoa, and offer the chance of hiking from one to another. One of the most popular is the Llullu Llama hostel in Isinliví (tel: 281-4790; www.isinlivi.safari.com. $$), which makes a point of being eco-friendly, with composting toilets and organic gardens. It has an agreeable, very communal atmosphere, with excellent organic food and mostly shared accommodations (some private rooms available). The Llullu Llama hostel is

close to the center of **Isinliví**. Ask to see the village workshop, which does some of the best commercial woodwork in Ecuador. If you would like to spend more time here, the hostel has maps of a variety of hiking trails in the vicinity.

Hike with a View

This hike southwest to Chugchilán, toward Quilotoa, takes up to 6 hours (usually less), so leave by 10am next morning. Take water and some food. The easiest option is to arrange with the hostel for a local farmer and horse, to show you the route and schlep your bag ($15–20). Ask to be taken on the high route via the suspension bridge across Toachi Canyon, which has the best views and variety of scenery. The first half of the hike is easy, with a thrill

Left: the village of Isinliví

or two at the somewhat rickety Toachi suspension bridge (at low water it is possible to wade across the river). Upstream on the west bank you pass through the village of **Itualo**, with a quaint country chapel, and then comes a fairly tough climb until you hit the road, where you turn left to **Chugchilán**.

The Black Sheep Inn (tel: 281-4587; www.blacksheepinn.com; $$$ including breakfast and dinner) at Chugchilán is signposted to the right before you reach the village. Owned by American eco-exiles, Andres Hammerman and Michelle Kirby, it is also very eco-friendly, and offers both shared and private accommodations (shared bathrooms), a welcoming atmosphere, wholesome food, tours, and activities. Closer to the village, Mama Hilda's hostel (tel: 281-4814; $$ including breakfast and dinner) is clean and comfortable. Budget accommodations are also available in Chugchilán.

Quilotoa Crater

It's possible to go by road to **Quilotoa crater** and do a 5-hour hike back to Chugchilán, on a sometimes tricky trail: spend an extra night in Chugchilán and visit the crater next day. One option is to take the bus to Zumbahua, which leaves at 4am, or take a taxi. ($15–20). By bus, make sure the driver knows you are getting off at Quilotoa. It's a short walk from the main road up to the crater rim, but this is a bleak, cold place, so bring warm clothes. Deposit your baggage at the Cabañas de Quilotoa hotel (return later for breakfast) then stroll up to the rim. The view into the crater is breathtaking and magnificent. You will be staring straight into the sunrise, so be there as the sun peeks over the rim. You can hike to the lake's edge, half an hour there and one hour back.

From Quilotoa you will need a taxi for the 12km (8 miles) to Zumbahua, where you can catch a bus back to Latacunga and Quito.

Above: at a schoolhouse north of Quilotoa
Right: abundant citrus fruit at Saquisilí market

central & southern highlands

9. BAÑOS AND TUNGURAHUA *(see map p44)*

Take a half-day ride from Quito and a day or two to enjoy the sub-tropical valley town of Baños, with lots of hiking and biking trails, soothing hot springs to soak in and nightlife.

Buses from Quito go through Ambato and take about 3½ hours. Departures are frequent. Take a morning bus – either the Baños or Expreso Baños lines, from the Terminal Terrestre – to be in Baños by lunchtime.

Baños is a spa, sports, vacation, and party town. With its warm climate, hot springs, and lovely mountain scenery, it is a place where many Quiteños get away and relax for a long weekend to cycle, hike, or hit the night spots. It was formerly a popular novice climber's destination, too, when **Tungurahua**, the 5,023-m (16,495-ft) volcano that looms over the town to the south, was a fairly easy glacier climb.

The Unquiet Earth

Not any more. In 1999 the volcano went into an active phase that culminated in the evacuation of the town later that year. However, there was no damage to Baños, and in early 2000 residents began returning. The volcano quietened a bit, and today it's business as usual, minus the hiking on the flanks below the crater, and the mountaineering; the locals are quite blasé about it all. Tungurahua's explosive force and debris spew westward, while Baños lies in the Pastaza valley to the northeast. Although things could change, many experts believe that at present Ambato and Riobamba are more vulnerable than Baños itself. Nonetheless, the government has built a large

Above: volcanic ash erupts from Tungurahua
Left: waterfall where Río Verde meets Río Pastaza

bridge over the river so that the town can be evacuated quickly in the event of a major new eruption. Meanwhile, Tungurahua frequently, though unpredictably, unleashes an epic belch, which can be seen from north of the Pastaza gorge.

Exploring Baños

The town is notably friendly and makes for a pleasant stroll, with palm-ringed squares, quiet streets, internet cabins and sidewalk cafés, and it's small enough to go everywhere in the center on foot. Food stands by the bus terminal sell sugar cane and *melcocha*, a very sweet local toffee.

If it's lunchtime, try a delicious Mexican taco at Pancho Villa (Montalvo y 16 de Diciembre), then consider renting a motorcycle or all-terrain-vehicle for a ride up to the *antenas* (radio masts) on a mountain top on the north bank of the Pastaza. You could hike, or even cycle this route, but it's a long, steep haul of at least 3 hours round-trip on foot. Several stores around the intersection of 16 de Diciembre y Martinez rent motorcycles and ATVs for about $10 per hour; choose a more powerful model (200–250cc) if there are two of you. Take a quick spin and check the brakes before renting.

The views of Baños and Tungurahua as you zigzag up the gravel road are stupendous. With luck you will witness an eruption of ash. At night the mountain sometimes glows under a rain of red-hot rocks. To check if Tungurahua is clear of cloud before renting your wheels, walk across the new San Francisco bridge on the Ambato highway opposite the bus station and continue until you can look back and see the volcano.

Curative Waters

Baños means 'baths,' so during your visit stroll down to the **Manto de la Virgen** (Virgin's Cloak), a high waterfall at the east end of town where the **municipal baths** (daily 4.30am–5, 6–10pm) are located. The brownish, mineral-rich waters are said to have curative properties. To avoid crowds go early morning, especially on weekends and public holidays. The people are very amiable and sociable, so it's also a good place to meet locals.

Believers say the true source of healing at the baths is Our Lady of the Holy Water, the Virgin of Baños, whose image is kept in the **Basilica** on Ambato y 12 de Noviembre. The Virgin is also said to protect the town from the volcano and to have performed prodigious miracles, paintings of which hang on the walls of the basilica. She is reputed to appear to devotees in dreams demanding they make her extravagant costumes; these can be seen in the **Sala de la Virgen** (Mon–Sat, 8am–4pm).

Above: the main public hot springs at Baños

When it's time for dinner, try one of the excellent steaks at the Cuisine de Provence (Halflants y Rocafuerte, tel: 274-0911), which represent great value for money. Afterwards if you're in the mood, head for the town's night spots, the Bamboo Bar for instance, which are clustered around Eloy Alfaro and Oriente.

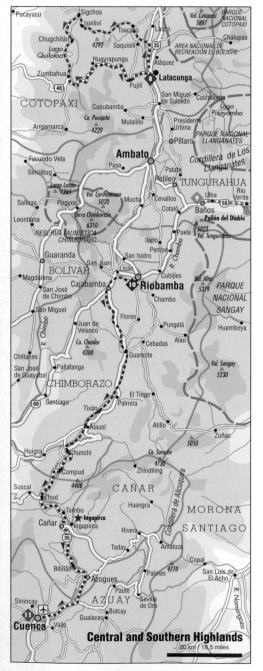

Central and Southern Highlands
30 km | 18.5 miles

Waterfalls and Río Verde

Downstream from Baños, many waterfalls drop into the gorge. The road to Puyo follows the left bank of the river, and one of the classic things to do is to rent a bicycle and ride as far as Río Verde, viewing the waterfalls along the way and ending with a walk to the climactic Pailón del Diablo falls. Bike rentals are widely available; try Adrian Carrillo, 12 de Noviembre y Martinez. Check the bike thoroughly: ride it and test the gears, brakes, and general condition. Make sure there is a helmet, lock, tire pump, and puncture repair kit.

Río Verde is only about 1½ hours downstream, so there's plenty of time to enjoy the scenery and birdlife along the way. Aim to be there for lunchtime. Go to the main highway, turn right and follow the road, which is mostly downhill and entirely paved. There are several tunnels, but it's safest to bypass these, following the old dirt road along the cliffside.

The village, to the right of the highway in a gap between two tunnels, is on the river of the same name. Leave the highway, follow the river downstream and cross the first bridge. Just ahead are two restaurants, and a trail leading down to the **Pailón del Diablo**. Leave your bike at one of the restaurants (tip them later), and walk for about 20 minutes beneath spectacular cliffs down the steep path to the falls. A small snack bar and restaurant here has a warm,

Right: tourists on the roof of a train from Riobamba to Alausí

jungly outdoor setting. A nearby balcony gets you close to the thundering falls, while a short trail down to a suspension bridge across the Pastaza gives an overview. You can cross the bridge and climb up the south bank of the river for another view.

If you feel like hiking in the area, there is a foot trail on the west bank of the Río Verde beyond the highway up a fairly steep valley through lovely woodland filled with wildflowers and bird life. To return to Baños flag down any bus on the highway, and stow your bike in the baggage hold.

To avoid speeding traffic, do this excursion as a hike on the south bank of the Pastaza. Take an urban bus in Baños from the corner of Eloy Alfaro and Martinez down the main highway to the bridge just before the Agoyán dam. Before the bridge (don't cross it) take the lower of two trails that lead downstream. Follow this, avoiding lesser turn-offs, for 2–3 hours to enjoy terrific views of the waterfalls on the north bank. At the **Manto de la Novia** falls a *tarabita* cable car will, for a small fee, carry you to the north bank. Flag a bus to take you back to Baños or onward to Río Verde, for the visit to the Pailón del Diablo. Allow 5–6 hours for the full trip.

You could continue on to the next itinerary by taking a bus to Riobamba via Ambato. The direct Baños-Riobamba highway, which still appears on most maps, has been cut by volcanic debris.

10. OVER THE DEVIL'S NOSE *(see map p44)*

Take two nights out of Quito, to ride the roof of a historic train from Riobamba over the Devil's Nose (El Nariz del Diablo) to Sibambe, continuing on to Ecuador's most impressive Inca ruins at Ingapirca.

Buses from Quito to Riobamba are frequent and take about 3½ hours. From there trains (Wed, Fri, and Sun; $11) leave at 7am (confirm with Riobamba station, 10 de Agosto and Carabobo, tel: 296-1909). Buy your ticket the previous day (ticket office open 4–about 8pm). Leave Quito the day before, to arrive around lunchtime.

In its heyday Ecuador's railroad system was a vital modernizing link between Quito, Guayaquil and the nation's major cities. But highway construction had railroads in decline by the 1970s, and the El Niño of 1982 caused so much

damage that they never recovered. One of the last sections still operating travels from Riobamba to Alausí and Sibambe over the Devil's Nose, a vertical mountain which caused nightmares for the railroad's late 19th-century builders. It's a fun ride – one of the few passenger trains in the world to consist mainly of freight cars; you almost *have* to ride on the roof (there is usually only one passenger car). The bucolic country scenes, the attractive old towns such as Guamote and Alausí, and the drama of the switchback ride over the Devil's Nose make this a trip well worth taking.

Two modest hotels are convenient for the train, the Tren Dorado (Carabobo 22–35 y 10 de Agosto; tel: 296-4890; $$) and Los Shyris (Rocafuerte 21–60 y 10 de Agosto, tel: 296-0323; $$). Hotel options at Ingapirca are somewhat limited, so for comfortable lodgings make a reservation ahead at the Posada Ingapirca (tel: 282-7401, Cuenca; www.grupo-santaana.com; $$$), an old *hacienda* hotel a 15-minute walk from the village. In the village, the best of several basic hotels is the Intihuasi ($).

Riobamba and the Devil's Nose

The afternoon is well spent viewing the downtown area of Riobamba, with its beautiful late-colonial and republican architecture. The facade of the **cathedral** on Parque la Libertad is worth seeing for its wealth of detailed stone carving, and across the park on the corner of Primera Constituyente and Benalcazar there are often temporary exhibitions at the Municipal Museum. The **Museo de las Conceptas** (Argentinos y Larrea; Mon–Sat 9am–noon, 3–6pm) displays ecclesiastical memorabilia and a famous treasure, a glittering solid gold and jewel-encrusted monstrance, in which the host is kept. In clear weather, plan to be at **La Loma de Quito**, the park at León and Orozco, as sunset approaches. You can see up to five of Ecuador's highest snowcapped volcanoes from here, in an arc from northwest to southeast in this order: Chimborazo, Carihuairazo, Tungurahua, Altar, and Sangay.

For the train ride, arrive at the station early (soon after 6am), bring warm clothing, raingear, and sunblock, and *do* rent one of the cushions offered at the station. Bring food for the journey, or take your chances on a trackside lunch at Guamote. Put your overnight bag in the baggage car (be sure to get a claim check) and carry what you need in a day pack. The rooftop ride is an exciting and eventful experience. Use a fast shutter speed for taking pictures from the moving train.

The train frequently derails, quite harmlessly, and it takes time to get going again, so the duration of the journey is unpredictable. Typically it ends around 2pm. You pass through Alausí and continue over the **Devil's Nose**, the most dramatic part of the trip, before returning to Alausí station.

Above: Cañari Indian women guides at Ingapirca

Leaving the station, turn right and go about one block to where a bus to Cuenca awaits the train. Ride this as far as Tambo, about 2 hours from Alausí, and ask the driver to stop at the main square.

The Ruins at Ingapirca

From Tambo a side road climbs to the village of **Ingapirca**, about 20 minutes' drive. Local buses take this route every 20 minutes or so, until around 6pm, or you can take a taxi to Ingapirca village (about $5 – a little extra to the Posada Ingapirca).

Ingapirca ruins (daily 8am–6pm; admission charge) are close to the village and the entrance ticket includes the small site **Museum** (daily 9am–5pm), and a guided tour (in Spanish, though some guides speak a little English); tipping is recommended. Ingapirca was taken over by the invading Incas from the conquered Cañari people of the region, for whom it seems to have been a sacred place. It is commonly described as a fortress, but that is the one thing it clearly is not. On the former Inca royal highway up the central Andes, it may have been designed to incorporate the Cañari site into the Inca religion. It has many of the features of a classical high-status Inca ceremonial center, with a commanding view of the landscape, a raised platform, baths, and carefully built terraces. The lozenge shape of the central platform is unique among surviving Inca structures. The raised platform may have been a sun temple, as this rounded form is often associated with the solar cult in Inca architecture. The structures are built in diorite, a highly workable stone quite similar to the stone of the Inca imperial capital at Cusco; the availability of this material might have influenced the Incas to choose this location.

Doubtless Ingapirca had secular functions, too. It was probably an

Above: the main tower at Ingapirca
Left: Ingapirca llama

administrative center for the Inca regional government, and possibly a royal *tambo*, or lodging on the highway. To observe the intricacies of Inca stonework inspect the hundreds of cut stones from ruined buildings, laid out in neat rows on the ground east of the main platform. A short walk of about 45 minutes, starting just west of the site, takes you past a series of enigmatic Inca rock carvings, starting with a bath *(Incachungana),* the "tortoise," the Inca's throne, and the Inca's eye, among others.

If continuing to Cuenca, buses leave from Ingapirca at 1.10pm and 4.10pm, arriving Cuenca at 3.30pm and 6.30pm. For Riobamba and Quito, return to Tambo by local bus and flag a northbound bus on the highway.

11. THE ATHENS OF ECUADOR: COLONIAL CUENCA
(see maps p44 and below)

The capital of the southern highlands and Ecuador's third-largest city, Cuenca is the country's jewel of colonial architecture.

Cuenca is a 10-hour bus journey from Quito, so unless traveling here in stages, you may prefer to take one of the frequent daily flights (see Getting Around, page 91).

The site of present-day Cuenca first appears in the historical record as a stronghold of the Cañari tribe, who controlled this part of Ecuador for a thousand years until the Incas conquered them in the late 15th century. The Incas liked this warm, sunny valley, and it became their northern capital for a time, until they advanced farther north and took Quito. Most of the Inca city has disappeared now, buried under the Spanish city founded in 1557. Colonial Cuenca, in a fertile farming valley, became a center for working precious metals in early colonial times. During the early republic

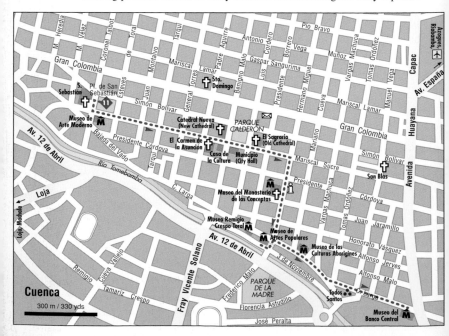

it became the capital of the third province, after Quito and Guayaquil, and it is still the nation's third-largest city. It has a reputation as the birthplace of many of Ecuador's best-known intellectuals and artists, hence its label, the 'Athens of Ecuador.' Yet Cuenca thrived in relative isolation from the rest of the country; the railroad did not reach here until 1965, long after Quito and the central highlands were connected to the coast, which perhaps helps to explain why Cuenca is still a rather staid and conservative city.

San Sebastián Square

Cuenca has outstanding colonial and republican buildings in its downtown area, listed as a Unesco World Heritage Site in 1999. Note that most churches tend to be closed except during hours of worship. There is a tourist information office in the city hall in Parque Calderón.

The following route will show you a broad sample of old Cuenca's architectural delights. Start at the west end of the city, in the spacious and elegant **San Sebastián Square**. The **Museo de Arte Moderno** (Museum of Modern Art; Mon–Fri 8.30am–6.30pm; Sat 9am–3pm; free) on the south side of the square is a colonial-style building with a labyrinth of galleries, patios, and gardens, housing a permanent collection of works by local artists, plus temporary exhibits which maintain a high standard. Make your way from here along Mariscal Sucre for four blocks, which brings you to the rear of the new cathedral at the corner of Padre Aguirre, where a morning flower market adorns the forecourt of the chapel of El Carmen. Another block along is the **Parque Calderón**, the beautiful and well-kept heart of the city, where the city hall, and both the new and old cathedrals are located. Con-

struction of the old cathedral – now the church of **El Sagrario** – on the east side of the square, was begun in 1557, the year of Cuenca's founding, and some of the stones of the Inca structure that once stood there can still be seen. In the early 1880s work was begun on the vast **Catedral Nueva** (New Cathedral) that fills the west side of the square. Holding up to 10,000 worshipers, with floors of Carrara marble from Italy, columns and steps of a local pink marble, and alabaster trim, it is altogether an imposing building. If something appears to be

Above: detail from a Cuenca chapel
Right: church doorway in Cuenca

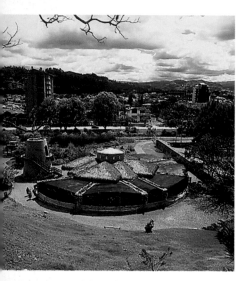

missing, something is; a miscalculation on the part of the otherwise-brilliant architect, a German priest, Johannes Stiehle, left the front towers unable to support the intended domes, or the bells that were to hang there, so they remain unfinished.

The **Casa de la Cultura** (Mon–Fri 9am–1pm & 3–6pm; free) in the southwest corner of the square, is an early colonial building which often houses temporary art exhibits.

City Museums

Continue two blocks on Mariscal Sucre and turn right on Hermano Miguel to reach the **Museo del Monasterio de las Conceptas** (Mon–Fri 9am–1pm & 2.30–5.30pm, Sat 9am–1pm; admission charge), housed in part of a cloistered convent founded in 1599. The museum displays many pieces of exceptionally fine folk and religious art, including a splendid nativity scene.

Continue down Hermano Miguel, cross Calle Larga, and go a short way down the steps leading to the Río Tomebamba. To the right, the Café Wunderbar offers good coffee, ice cream, pastries, and a place to relax. You are at the so-called 'cliff' of Cuenca, the steep bank below Calle Larga, atop which sits some of Cuenca's most desirable real estate.

Return to Calle Larga and head right for half a block for a visit to the **Museo de las Culturas Aborígenes** (tel: 283-9181; Mon–Fri 8.30am–6.30pm, Sat 8.30am–1pm; admission charge). This private museum, founded by local historian Dr Juan Cordero, has an intimate and personal flavor that few museums can match, with an orchid-filled patio, an excellent museum shop, and a wealth of objects from the diverse cultures that populated the Cuenca region before the Spanish conquest. Six blocks along, at Calle Larga 1–279, the El Maíz Restaurant (tel: 284-0224) serves a variety of typical Ecuadorean dishes, under the enthusiastic direction of owner-chef Eulalia Blaudín.

One more block down Larga brings you to the blockhouse-modern building of the national bank, at the far end of which is the **Museo del Banco Central** (Mon–Fri 9am–6pm, Sat 9am–1pm; admission charge). The museum features a small collection of artifacts excavated from the Inca ruins of Pumapungo, in a quiet park behind the bank (admission includes entrance to the park). There are a number of fine exhibits of Ecuadorean ethnic costume and daily life, plus a climactically displayed collection of

Above: view over the park of the Museo del Banco Central with the aviary at the center

central & southern highlands

shrunken heads from the Amazon. There are also colonial and republican art galleries, and, not surprisingly, a fulsome coin and banknote collection. The Inca structures in the park consist of foundations and reconstructions, and there are good views over south Cuenca and the river, spacious gardens and ponds, and an aviary of native birds.

In good weather, top off the day with a panoramic view of Cuenca from **El Turi**, a viewpoint on a hill south of the town with a church atop it and a large ceramic map of the city to tell you what you are looking at.

Pots and Hats

Take a taxi and keep it with you while you visit, a short way back down the highway, the workshop of **Eduardo Vega**, one of Ecuador's best-known ceramic artists. Then head back into the center to see how Panama hats are made. As most people now know, these are not from Panama. Travelers in the 19th century used to buy them there, hence the name, but they were imported from Ecuador. Cuenca's most famous hatter is Homero Ortega & Sons (Gil Ramírez Dávalos 386, tel: 280-9000; weekdays 9am–noon & 3–6pm; free), near both the airport and the main bus station. They offer a tour through the complex processes of their trade, hoping, of course, to sell you a hat. This is an interesting stop on your way in or out of town.

Cajas National Park

Those who come to Ecuador for the outdoors will not be disappointed by a visit to **Parque Nacional El Cajas** (admission charge), the source of Cuenca's rivers. It also has more than 275 lakes, good trout fishing, hiking, and bird-watching and is very accessible – less than an hour by bus, with frequent departures. Trails are not well marked, and the area is full of ridges and shrub thickets, so hiking requires a good sense of direction. Being fairly high, the area calls for warm clothes and raingear. To stay overnight, an organized visit is recommended *(see Useful Addresses, page 98).*

Above: vendor of medicinal herbs, Cuenca
Left: figure of a shaman in the Museo de las Culturas Aborígenes

The Coast

Before the Amazon oil boom the coast was the main locomotive of Ecuador's economy, exporting cacao, timber, cotton, coffee, tropical fruits, fish and farmed shrimp, and of course, bananas. Even *tagua* – 'vegetable ivory' – and *toquilla*, the palm frond used to make Panama hats, play a small but significant role in the diverse life of this region, which is home to half the nation's population. Ecuador's earliest civilizations arose here, too, and coastal culture is still rich, varied, and distinct, with descendants of slaves predominant in the north, a paradoxical mix of tropical languor and bustle in the cities, indigenous rainforest tribes besieged by modern civilization in the north, and *montuvio* fishing and farming lifestyles everywhere.

Four cities dominate: Esmeraldas, once a center of emerald trading – hence its name – is now the major northern port, the outlet for the trans-Andean oil pipeline and shipping point for a major new logging industry. Farther south, Manta is an important fishing port, with the most pleasant climate, while Guayaquil, located on the steamy estuary of the Guayas River, is the nation's first port and largest city. Machala, in the south, is the nation's banana capital. All except Machala have good beach life nearby – along with archeological sites, mangrove inlets and some distinctive forest environments.

Coastal climates

In the extreme north and south the Andes fall steeply to coastal plain and then ocean, while the central coast is bounded by a secondary range of foothills, which frequently touch the shore. A bewildering range of micro-climates prevails, though few people agree about what and where they are. Broadly speaking, however, two climates mirror one another, north and south, dividing roughly at the Río Chone. The north is sunny from May through October, and can be very rainy January through March. In the south, the sunny season is December through to the end of April, while June through October can be quite cloudy and humid. High tourist season goes with the sunshine in each region. Beach resorts near big cities are crowded at weekends.

Until the modern era, diseases like yellow fever and malaria took a fearful toll on the tropical coast, stunting the growth of urban centers, and giving it a bad reputation among travelers. The situation is vastly improved today, though visitors should be aware of some specific medical and security issues (*see Health and Emergencies, pages 88 and 96–7*).

Left: Los Frailes beach, in Machaililla National Park
Right: indigenous guide from the Aqua Binca community

12. THE MONTUVIO COAST *(see map p56)*

The Andes plunge toward the Pacific just west of Quito and other highland cities, taking the traveler into another world. From the rainy tropical north, via endless deserted beaches, to the teeming bustle of Guayaquil, Ecuador's coast is a traveler's feast.

You will need a car for this route. There are opportunities for a dip in the ocean, so bring swimming gear and sun block. Note, however, that there are some strong currents in places; enquire locally about safety. Bring suitable footwear for nature walks. The big resorts get busy on weekends, so choose a weekday if you prefer peace and quiet.

Esmeraldas is the capital of the north coast, of Afro-Ecuador, and of the African-influenced dance music played on the xylophone-like palmwood instrument, the *marimba*. Easily accessible by road or air from Quito, most coast-bound visitors prefer to escape Esmeraldas' ruckus, grime and crime, perhaps by taking the coast road northeast to sleepy Rio Verde or Las Peñas, for a quiet getaway on the beach. Following this coast, the road dead-ends at **La Tola**, where the offshore island of La Tolita once harbored an opulent civilization, famous for its elaborate goldwork that has either been looted or is today kept in distant museums.

Around Esmeraldas

The main highway goes inland via Borbón to steamy **San Lorenzo**, also reachable by road from the highland town of Ibarra. Smaller and calmer than Esmeraldas, it's probably the best spot to soak up Afro-Ecuadorean culture and hear *marimba*. It's also a jumping-off point for excursions into nearby ecological reserves, which include coastal mangrove forests, and the threatened rainforest of this area.

Just southwest of Esmeraldas lies the resort of **Atacames**, famous (or perhaps notorious) for its round-the-clock party and disco atmosphere. A stone's throw farther west, the fishing village of **Sua** is extremely pleasant and much quieter. Then, 100km (60 miles) southwest of Esmeraldas is the island of **Muisné**, a tranquil, practically car-free, laid-back town. Stay at the beach end, and enjoy the local *cocada* seafood dishes – fish and shell-fish cooked in a spicy coconut sauce.

In and Around Manta

Manta is a major fishing and commercial port, somewhat sanitized since a US airbase was built there. It has a year-round sunny microclimate, a lively beachfront boulevard to the west, and the funky fishing harbor of Tarqui to the east. Manta was a center of the prehispanic Manteño culture, which developed and controlled maritime trade along the Pacific coast. Don't miss the **Museo del Banco Central**, with its excellent archeological exhibits. Just inland from Manta, you can enjoy the genteel decay of **Montecristi**, once a thriving center of the Panama hat trade *(see pages 51 and 77)*, and still a good place to buy one.

North of Manta lies the coastal village of **Crucita**, with good beaches and optimal paragliding conditions – a good place to get a tandem ride to try this sport. Farther north lies **Bahía de Caráquez**, a city with a population of 25,000 on the broad Río Chone estuary. The destructive El Niño of 1998, plus a severe earthquake, prompted its reconstruction as an environmentally sound 'eco-city.' Despite mangrove degradation by shrimp farms, it's a good base for the conservation-minded visitor to observe permaculture and restoration projects in action, and to visit surviving mangrove and dry tropical forest. The **Saiananda Zoo-Botanical Reserve** near Bahía, and the **Río Muchacho Organic Farm and Lodge** north of Canoa (www.riomuchacho.com) are recommended excursions.

Crossing the Chone estuary to **San Vicente** by car ferry or motorboat, there's an unbroken 17-km (10 ½-mile) stretch of beach that can be walked all the way to Canoa (alternatively, there is a bus service). The beach has good surfing, especially between the months of December and April.

The Ruta del Sol

South of Salango at **Puerto Rico** is a famous ecological community and lodge, the **Hosteria Alandaluz** (www.alandaluz.com), where you can wander around organic gardens on the beach (strong surf; not ideal swimming), and take nature-wildlife walks up into the **Chongón-Colonche** coastal range within the **Cantalapiedra** private reserve.

From here a string of villages and beaches stretches southward along the 'Ruta del Sol,' some of them with heavy surf and currents, so use caution when swimming. The beach village of **Olón** has some facilities for visitors. **Montañita**, with its excellent waves, is the crowded and chaotic surfing

Left: playing football on the beach at Atacames
Right: Guayaquil on the Guayas River

The Coast
50 km / 31 miles

PACIFIC

OCEAN

Equator

capital of Ecuador. **Manglaralto**, a larger but still pleasant town with good beaches, specializes in growing and carving *tagua* – elephant-friendly 'vegetable ivory' – used to make everything from buttons to artistic carvings. South from here, approaching the Santa Elena peninsula, the landscape gradually becomes arid scrub-desert.

Guayaquil and Beyond

Guayaquil, Ecuador's main port and biggest city, is the south-central coast's major center. Its tropical-metropolis frenzy, high crime, and dearth of attractions made it a place to avoid in the past, but municipal efforts to clean it all up and attract tourism have had some success. The riverfront *malecón,* with new parks and restaurants, makes a great after-noon stroll, while three blocks inland, 'Iguana Park,' actually **Parque Bolívar**, entertains visitors and locals alike with its thriving reptile population and botanical gardens. The hilly bohemian district of **Las Peñas** is a friendly place with old wooden architecture and artistic graffiti – it's also a good place to buy a painting.

Southwest of Guayaquil lies the lumpen beach resort of **Playas**, which is absolutely packed on weekends, while farther west, the fishing village of **Chanduy** has important archeological remains and a museum, the **Museo Real Alto** (Tues–Sun 9am–5pm; admission charge). At **Santa Elena**, a very ancient cemetery of the Las Vegas culture features the famous skeletons of an embracing couple in the **Museo de los Amantes de Sumpa** (Mon–Sat 9am–4pm, Sun 10am–3pm; admission charge). At the far end of the peninsula lies **Salinas**, the overpriced, overcrowded, indispensable beach resort for everybody who's anybody in Guayaquil.

13. PUERTO LOPEZ AND ISLA DE LA PLATA *(see map left)*

Take three or more nights out of Quito to visit the fishing port of Puerto López, the Isla de la Plata, and Parque Nacional Machalilla.

Visit between mid-June and September if you want to see the humpback whales, or at any other time if you want sunny beach weather. If you have them, bring along a mask and fins for snorkeling. There's a fast, reasonably comfortable overnight bus from the Reina del Camino terminal (tel: 257-2673) in the new city at 18 de Septiembre y Manuel Larrea. Depart at 8pm and arrive about 6am. Try to get a middle or rear seat, away from the blaring music that keeps the driver awake. Traveling this way leaves time to check in to a hotel and take a boat tour at around 9am. A softer, but more costly and time-consuming way, is to fly to Manta and take a bus to Puerto López.

The main center of the area, **Puerto López** is mainly a fishing port but it is being developed for tourism. A recommended hotel in the town is the Hostería Mandala (tel: 230-0181 www.hosteriamandala.com; $$), at the north end of Puerto López beach. Owners Aurelio Cipriani and Maja Steiner are welcoming hosts. Guests stay in individual cabins in lush, tropical gardens, and the place has many droll touches reflecting their creativity.

In front of the hotel the owners have created an outdoor **Whale Museum**, assembling the skeleton of a large male humpback whale found dead on a remote beach. This location is also handy for a photogenic visit to the fisherman's market where boats bring in their nightly catch around 10am.

Getting around Puerto López is cheap, easy and fun. Motor-tricycle taxis will take you anywhere within the town for 25¢. Negotiate the price for a longer journey.

Above: showing off the catch, Puerto López
Right: blue-footed boobies on Isla de la Plata

Boat tours leave from *el malecón,* the beachfront boulevard where most of the restaurants and tour offices are located. Machalilla Tours (tel: 230-0206) and Exploramar Diving (tel: 230-0123; www.exploradiving.com) both have offices on the *malecón,* and are recommended (the latter is the only PADI-certified dive shop here). Beware of unlicensed fishing boats offering discount tours; there will be no lifejacket, no toilet, and no security. The sea can be choppy, so you may need to take a sea sickness remedy.

In whale season, the tour will scout for whales all the way to Isla de la Plata *(see page 58)* and back, and the chances of seeing them are very good. You may see mothers with their calves, and courtship displays of breaching, fin-pointing, and tail-waving. During the 2004 season, some 500 individual whales were identified here.

Puerto López has plenty of other recreational activities: there are good dive sites, and you can take a diving course here. Surfing is good at Las Tunas and Río Chico beaches, and boards can be rented. (Hardcore surfers gather at Montañita, farther south.) The aforementioned agencies also offer deep-sea fishing for mahi mahi, tuna, and other game species.

Machalilla National Park

The 55,000-hectare (136,000-acre) **Machalilla National Park** (admission charge; pay at park office in Puerto López or to a park ranger) and its surroundings, on the coast southeast of Quito, has numerous attractions for visitors. If planning to visit the land portion of the park and the Isla de la Plata *(see below),* purchase the combined park ticket, valid for one week, thereby saving some money. The main event of the year is the arrival of the humpback

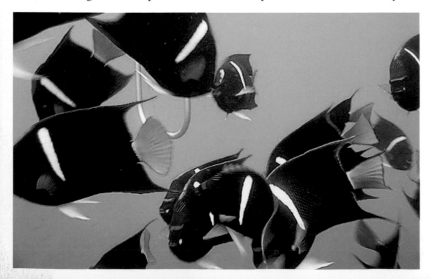

whales, around mid-June. These magnificent creatures remain in the area until the end of September, courting and calving in the shallow waters offshore.

Land-based attractions include hiking through the coastal cloud forest, with wild orchids and other tropical plants. Some trips within the park are included in the park fee, but you may have to pay an additional charge for visiting the cloud forest area.

Poor Man's Galápagos

The **Isla de la Plata**, some 50km (30 miles) offshore, lies at the heart of the 35,000-hectare (86,500-acre) marine sector of the national park. If you are only visiting the island and not venturing into the landward part of the park, you will just pay a partial park fee. Here you will find large numbers of nesting birds, such as blue-footed and masked boobies, frigate birds, and even a few waved albatrosses. Because of this, the island has gained the soubriquet 'the poor man's Galápagos'. However, it is actually very different. The geology is formed of sedimentary rock, not volcanic, and the plant species here correspond with similar environments on the mainland.

The island has a history. Evidence that it was sacred to the Manteño culture has been unearthed, and later the Incas performed ritual sacrifices there. Pirates anchored off the island in colonial times, and rumors of buried treasure still circulate – indeed, Isla de la Plata translates as 'silver island.'

Isla de la Plata is a wild, arid place of towering cliffs, with no permanent residents other than the seabirds. There are some good trails that you can follow – always with the park guide who accompanies your tour.

Tours generally end with snorkeling off one of the island's rocky shores. The water is quite warm here, and no wet suit is necessary. An excursion taking in whale-watching, landing on the island, and taking a dip in the ocean makes a full and satisfying day.

Salango

If you have extra time for further exploration of the coast, set out for the little village of **Salango**, a short way south along the coast road. There's a regular bus service (the journey takes about 15 minutes), but it's most fun to take a motor-trike and stop along the way at the lookout over the bay on the climb out of Puerto López. Aim to arrive in time for lunch at the Delfín Mágico restaurant, which serves good seafood; the *spondylus al ajillo,* a dish based on the famous spiny oyster found in the region, is a great specialty.

Salango is the location of an important archeological excavation revealing evidence of a 5,000-year-old settlement. The museum, the **Balseros del Mar del Sur** (daily 3.30–6pm; admission charge) in the village center, has good background information about the region before the Spanish conquest.

Above Left: tourists at Isla de la Plata **Left:** king angelfish off Isla de la Plata
Right: assembling a whale skeleton for an open-air exhibition

14. LOS FRAILES AND AGUA BLANCA *(see map p56)*

A day trip out of Puerto López to the superb white-sand beach of Los Frailes in the morning, then Agua Blanca and a living archeological site in the afternoon. Return to Quito via the varied scenery of the new coast road to Manta.

Hire a motor-trike and driver ($15–20 for the day, and you pay at the end). Take water and a packed lunch (nothing is available on the beach), swimming gear, and sun block.

The road north of Puerto López goes into the heart of **Machalilla National Park** *(see page 58)*, which protects some of Ecuador's finest beaches from any kind of development – not even camping is allowed here. Even during the cloudy months, this area's microclimate is sunny more often than Puerto López.

Los Frailes Beach

There are three beaches on a series of rocky points about 11km (7 miles) from Puerto López. After a slow, breezy and usually quite delightful ride – on one section, carob trees form a cool green tunnel over the highway – you will arrive at the park entrance (bring your ticket, or pay when you get here), about 1km (²/₃ mile) walk from Los Frailes. Decide whether to complete the trail or return here, then arrange a rendezvous time and place with your ride, who may want to go somewhere else for a while.

Above: alone on Los Frailes beach
Left: a "panama" hat maker at Pile

the coast

Los Frailes is a magnificent crescent of wild, open beach, most secluded at the south end, with superb swimming (safest at the sheltered ends, away from the middle). Beware of manzanillo, more of an irritant than poison ivy, growing along the edge of the beach. A trail climbs from the north end of Los Frailes over a headland, where there is a side trail to a lookout platform, then on to the next beach, **Playa Arena Negra**, and continues to another, **La Tortugita**, where there is excellent snorkeling along the rocky point. The varied scenery of the beaches and headlands is memorable. Follow the trail to another park entrance farther north, or return to Los Frailes.

Cultural Agua Blanca

Return south on the highway, and take the left-hand turn, signposted to Agua Blanca, where a road runs inland about 5km (3 miles) through a dry coastal forest area to this village. This is a cultural-archeological-ecological visit, and in many ways **Agua Blanca** seems a model of what cultural tourism should be. It's home to a proud indigenous community who live simple but dignified lives. Their village is clean and pleasant, the people are healthy and the children don't beg. Tourism here is like the river that runs through the village: the flow is modest but it never dries up, and it sustains their lives. There's a small entry fee, aside from the park fee, which includes a guided visit to their **Archeological Museum**, displaying artifacts from five ancient cultures dating back to 3,000BC who have lived on this spot, and a walking circuit that includes some ruins of the Manteño civilization, from whom the people of the village are most directly descended. This culminates in a bathing pool whose cool sulfur waters and oozing mud are said to have healing properties, and are deliciously welcome after a long, hot walk. Birdwatchers have plenty to see here. The dazzling blue-crowned mot-mot is common, and easy to spot. If it's lunchtime, El Barquito has a good, inexpensive set lunch. It's possible to stay at the village in one of the simple hotels. The San Antonio ($) is recommended.

For a longer stay here, it's possible to take a one- or two-day horseback or hiking trip into the mountains to the east, where the humid cloudforest environment is radically different, and there's a variety of tropical birds and monkeys. It is possible to set this up in Agua Blanca, or through one of the tour agencies in Puerto López.

When returning to Quito from Puerto López, you can take the paved coast road passing through Puerto de Cayo, and heading north from there (the standard route goes inland, through Jipijapa and Montecristi). It's a very scenic ride which stays near the shore most of the way, through scenery ranging from farmland, banana plantations, and lush coastal forest to arid scrub desert. A taxi (about $50) will allow you to stop at coastal villages, such as **Pile** (pronounced 'pea-lay'), where people still make Panama hats. Buses of the Cooperativa Manta also take this route, leaving every 2 hours, for a 2½-hour journey. From Manta you can either fly or take a bus back to Quito.

Right: ceramic vessel from the Archeological Museum at Agua Blanca

Oriente

They call it el Oriente – the East. This vast, forested region, largely ignored by mainstream Ecuador until oil was discovered in the 1960s, has changed dramatically since then. Today roads and pipelines criss-cross the region, oil towns have mushroomed, forest tracts have been razed, and indigenous lands invaded by colonists.

Yet huge areas of rainforest remain, some of it protected, and the best way to see it is by taking an organized trip there, perhaps to visit an eco-lodge. Some of these specialize in ecology, others focus more on contact with native groups, most offer some of both. All require advance reservations.

Both natural and human populations of the rainforest are under threat; contact with either should be careful and respectful; never buy products made from animal skins, feathers, etc. Recommended lodges maintain good environmental and cultural practices, train local guides, and share their income with native communities who, incidentally, wear Western-style clothes. The feathers and face-paint in which they are so often portrayed in the brochures is traditional dress that's reserved for ceremonial occasions.

Operating in remote areas is costly, and so, therefore, are rainforest tours. Nevertheless, the level of comfort and amenities varies greatly. Prices reflect, among other factors, the quality of guiding and environmental standards. A good guide is essential to appreciation of the rainforest, since it can be a featureless mass of vegetation to the untrained eye. Wildlife is usually elusive; in areas of colonization it is scarce; thus the remoter, more costly lodges also offer better wildlife viewing.

Travelers to the Oriente should carry passports (*see pages 88 and 96 for special health considerations*). Expect some biting insects, though some areas are worse than others. Lengthy boat rides are a feature of most visits, and can be fascinating in themselves. Carry insect repellent, sunblock, swimwear, broad-brim hat, and loose cotton clothes: long pants and long-sleeve shirts. During rainstorms boat rides get surprisingly chilly, so carry a windbreaker and sweater.

National parks and indigenous reserves invariably levy a fee for tourists, usually charged separately from the costs of a tour. Some quotes include cost of transportation from Quito and/or local taxes, others do not. Be clear about what is and is not included before signing up. It often takes an entire day each way to access the lodge, and tour itineraries include this, so you could get less rainforest time than you were expecting.

Left: view of the rainforest near the Río Napa
Right: dugout canoe ride down a jungle river

15. FOREST, WILDLIFE AND TRIBAL LANDS *(see map below)*

You need four or five days to get a true taste of the complex Amazonian ecosystems that are the focus of this itinerary.

It's a short flight or an 11-hour bus ride from Quito to Lago Agrio. Reserve accommodations and organize transportation to your chosen lodge from Lago Agrio. Take insect repellent and suitable clothing for forest walking.

Lago Agrio, the base for this tour, is an oil town on the Río Aguarico. North of the river in northern Ecuador, the Cuyabeno Reserve lies within

tribal lands of the Secoya and Siona people. The Cofán people, residing downriver within their own protected reserve, have set up their own ecotourism lodge, and have set out a trail system with guides (www.cofan.org).

The **Reserva Faunística Cuyabeno** (Biological Reserve) is an area of lakes and flooded forest. Wildlife viewing is good, and it's a prime location for spotting river dolphins, manatees and anacondas. From Lago Agrio it is a 3-hour drive to the Río Cuyabeno and a boat ride into the reserve.

The Cuyabeno Lodge (tel: 252-1212; www.neotropicturis.com), a mid-price lodge situated in the heart of the reserve, is recommended.

Above: a local Quicha guide

Yasuni and the Río Napo

Farther south, the nation's major Amazon tributary is the **Río Napo**, on whose lower reaches lies **Parque Nacional Yasuní** (Yasuní National Park). Home to the Huaorani Indians, it is of great interest to both conservationists and, unfortunately, oil companies. Access is via **Coca**, a remote oil town; road access is a possibility, but flying is highly recommended. Several good lodges operate downriver from Coca. At the high end is the **Napo Wildlife Center** (www.tropicalnaturetravel.com), owned and operated by the Quichua people. They do not take bookings from independent travelers, so call 289-7316 in Quito for a recommended booking agency. **Sacha Lodge** (tel: 256-6090, Quito; www.sachalodge.com), in the same general area, is a favorite with birders. Both these lodges have several prime ingredients of rainforest enjoyment: a tower for canopy viewing, a 'clay lick' where parrots and macaws gather in vast numbers, and a lake frequented by rare giant otters. **Bataburo Lodge** (tel: 250-5599; www.kempery.com), a mid-price lodge in Yasuní, offers contact with the Huaorani, good wildlife, and a canopy tower.

The top end is **Kapawi Eco Lodge** (www.kapawi.com), on the lower Río Pastaza, near the Peruvian border, far from colonists or oil wells. Access to this most isolated of rainforest lodges is by light aircraft. The operators work with the local Achuar, who will eventually own and run it. Wildlife and cultural aspects are good, and it's luxurious and eco-friendly, and priced accordingly.

Tena and the Upper Napo

The area around **Tena** on the upper Napo offers a less expensive alternative for rainforest visits. Tena and nearby **Misahuallí** are accessible by road, and jungle visits can be arranged from either town. Since the area is not isolated, large animals are elusive and rare, though you may see monkeys. Birds and butterflies are abundant. Tena has whitewater rafting and kayaking on the river; **River People** (tel: 288-8349) are recommended outfitters. Misahuallí is a sort of miniature Baños in the rainforest, devoted almost exclusively to tourism and partying, with many opportunities for excursions into the rainforest.

On the south bank of the upper Napo, the Huaorani coexist uneasily with oil companies, which allow only oil workers and Huaorani to operate in the area, and a few tourists. Within this zone, **Gareno Lodge** (tel: 234-4350, Quito; www.guaponi.com), a 2½-hour journey by road from Tena, offers a low-cost option of hikes and river trips through pristine rainforest, plus the unusual experience of driving through it in places, with no signs of human settlement. Wildlife is plentiful, but the Huaorani do hunt so mammals are scarce.

Right: an orchid at Gareno Lodge

The Galápagos
Islands

They are deceptive, these islands. Early Spanish sailors called them the Encantadas (Enchanted) islands because ever-shifting winds and currents and sudden fog made entire islands seem abruptly to appear or vanish. On land they still deceive, with an appearance of arid sameness which, when closely observed, quickly dissolves into astonishing variety.

Created by volcanic action 1–3 million years ago, the islands have highland zones of lush vegetation around cloud-shrouded peaks, while shorelines and the low ground are arid semi-desert. On the western edge of the archipelago newer volcanoes frequently spew lava; the islands are a geological work-in-progress. The cold, nutrient-rich waters of the Humboldt current flow through the islands, merging with warm equatorial waters in a turbulent mix of marine and land ecologies. Scattered along the coasts, tidal lagoons, brackish oases, lava fields, sandy beaches, and mangrove inlets generate their own singular environments.

Thousands of years ago the first land creatures arrived on rafts of floating vegetation from the Ecuadorean mainland. Reptiles survived the journey, but mammals could not, and there are almost no endemic land mammals here. Seabirds arrived in droves, of course, along with some landbirds, and adapted to the special conditions and absence of predators by losing their ability to fly, or by diverging from one species into numerous offshoots. One island has become the world's only significant nesting site of an entire species, the waved albatross. The ocean environment is equally abundant and varied, featuring numerous endemic species, including the unique marine iguana.

Humans may have discovered the islands earlier, but the first recorded visit was in 1535, when the Bishop of Panama's ship was blown off course on its way to Peru. Thereafter the islands became a base for pirates. In the 19th century, they became a favorite port of call for whalers, who carried off thousands of giant tortoises, driving some species into extinction.

In 1835 the survey ship HMS *Beagle* arrived to map the islands, enabling one passernger, the naturalist Charles Darwin, to spend five weeks there. This momentous visit would alter forever our view of nature and human development, as Darwin formulated his theory of evolution through natural selection, at the time a radical proposition.

Today the islands are faced with multiple conservation threats, both natural (El Niño) and man-made (overfishing, introduction of animals, tourism). A Unesco World Heritage Site since 1978, all of Galápagos – land and ocean – is theoretically protected, but there's a resident population of some 20,000 and pressure on resources threatens the inherently fragile environments. Attempts to balance competing forces is difficult, but visitors will be impressed with the level of control and protection that operates wherever tourists are allowed.

Left: mother sealion with pup, Puerto Egas, San Salvador
Right: flightless cormorant, Punta Espinoza, Fernandina

16. A Galápagos Cruise *(see map below)*

Follow in the wake of Charles Darwin for an eco-experience of a lifetime, and get a close-up (but don't touch) view of the islands' rich wildlife in the company of a knowledgable guide.

Most visitors take a pre-booked boat cruise through the islands, lasting one week. All visitors must present their passports and an entry fee of $100 (in cash only) on arrival in Galápagos. Flights from the mainland are currently $333–390 for a return trip for foreign visitors. TAME *(see* Getting Around, page 91*) flies to Baltra, on the north shore of Isla Santa Cruz, and from there you can either take a bus to Puerto Ayora, or meet up with your cruise operator. Take a hat, good sunglasses, plenty of sun block, louds of film, spare camera batteries, tough walking sneakers, swimming gear, and warm clothes. Arrange wet-suit rental, but bring your own mask, snorkel, and fins. Travel light – most boats have limited storage. If prone to seasickness pick up some* Mareol *from any Ecuadorean pharmacy.*

Cruises to the Galápagos follow a variety of itineraries set by the park service; some islands feature in virtually all itineraries, while others will figure according to their current status as visitor sites, and on the speed and range of the individual boat. No cruise visits all the islands. Crossings can be rough, especially in the southern sector from August through November, and are worst when traveling in a small boat. Some landings can be tricky in heavy seas. There are dry landings, on rocky shores and quays, and wet ones where you wade ashore on beaches. Some walks are moderately difficult: like much of the Ecuador experience, getting the most out of Galápagos requires a reasonable degree of physical fitness.

These days the better boats carry ocean kayaks for paddling around the shores, adding a bit of variety to the visit. Sport fishing is prohibited.

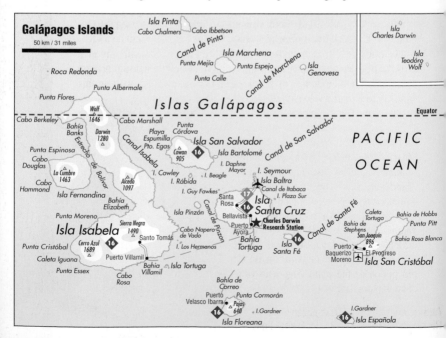

Choosing a Cruise

Your choice of boat depends on your budget and the kind of experience you want. Companies like Metropolitan Touring *(see useful addresses, page 99)* operate fast luxury ships accommodating around 100 passengers (who land in smaller groups), which can reach the more distant islands, but offer a less personal experience. More expensive ships are comfortable and spacious, and usually serve excellent food; smaller boats offer a more intimate cruise, but cheap boats can be slow and pretty basic, with guides who only speak Spanish.

Your guide will make a huge difference to your experience, because Galápagos cannot be fully appreciated without lots of information. The Darwin Research Station gives ratings to local guides: Class 1 speak only Spanish and offer land-based day tours; Class 2 are bilingual (Spanish and one other language, usually English) and have full guide training but no university education (some are very good because of personality and enthusiasm); Class 3 are university educated and have two or more languages (these guides usually accompany the luxury cruises).

Some people fly to Galápagos and book a boat when they get there *(see below)*. When booking in Quito, especially if you're looking for a last-minute special price, a good option is Safari Tours *(see Useful Addresses, page 98)*. They maintain a list of boats of varying prices, supply a wealth of information, and will not book you on a boat they do not personally recommend. They can sometimes get you up to 50 percent discount on a high-end boat for a last-minute booking, although cheaper boats will only give a 10–15 percent discount. Be extremely cautious about booking through obscure Ecuador-based tour agencies, as various scams are at work in this area. Try to get some reliable references besides their own assurances.

Setting Out

Most cruises begin with an airport pickup at **Baltra**. Just north lies the island of **Seymour**. Big land iguanas are common here, and blue-footed boobies rub shoulders with their tormentors, the magnificent frigate birds. These winged raiders have a major nesting site here. You can usually observe the inflated red pouch of the male frigate in full courtship display.

Above: cruising between the islands
Right: snorkeling with a turtle, Puerto Egas

East and South of Santa Cruz

Off the east coast of the major island of Santa Cruz, a favorite destination is **South Plaza** (Plaza Sur), where a windswept lava uplift covered in *sesuvium* succulents and large, flat *opuntia* cactus ends abruptly in a dramatic cliff, from whose edge you can look down upon swallow-tail gulls and red-billed tropic birds sporting above the surf. At the east end of the walking circuit is a bachelor club of unattached male sea lions. Large bull sharks have begun preying on the sea-lion colony here, curtailing snorkeling in the vicinity.

Southeast of Santa Cruz lies **Santa Fé**, whose small anchorage is one of the prettiest spots in the archipelago. Take the trail that climbs the fault cliff overlooking the southern half of the bay; here you can see the large land iguanas endemic to this island. Another trail is a short walk from the beach through an unusually tall forest of *opuntia* cactus. Snorkeling is excellent, and this is a good spot to swim with the (quite harmless) white-tipped reef shark. This island is frequented by day visitors from Puerto Ayora, so many of the cruise boats skip it.

The southernmost island is **Española** (Hood), a popular destination, since it is the world's only significant nesting site of the waved albatross. This graceful bird performs a bizarre and wonderful courtship dance involving sky-pointing, bowing, rocking, beak-swordplay, and mutual preening. Another booby species, the larger and more elegant masked booby, is abundant, and the local variety of marine iguanas turns an appealing blotchy red during the mating season. The island also features a blow-hole which sends up spectacular water spouts.

Sailing Westward

Turning west, the island of **Floreana** has several attractions, including the white-sand beach of Punta Cormorán, where turtles nest and the swimming is superb. In the nearby lagoon, shocking pink flamingoes light up the arid landscape. Offshore, a collapsed caldera known as the Devil's Crown offers superb snorkeling, although currents are strong and the water is often very cold. Also on the north shore, Bahía de Correo (Post Office Bay) features a famous barrel where 19th-century whalers dropped off and picked up their mail. Now surrounded by a motley collection of license plates and hand-painted signs, the barrel still invites tourists to collect and mail postcards with destinations near their homes, while leaving theirs for others to mail.

Farther west lies the archipelago's largest island, **Isabela**. Slower boats do not visit this island, since the popular sites are far out on the western shore. If your tour includes this outer island, consider it a plus; visitor sites are less crowded, and at sea you might see humpback, sperm, or even blue

Above: marine iguanas sunning themselves, Punta Espinosa
Above Right: Sally Lightfoot crab   **Right:** visiting Pinnacle Rock, Bartolomé island

whales. The area is also home to the unique flightless cormorant, an endemic species which abandoned flight due to the absence of predators. Popular landings are the lava field at Punta Moreno, suitable for an extended walk, skirting reed-filled oases with cloud-capped Cerro Azul volcano in the distance; Elizabeth Bay (Bahía Elizabeth), where a mangrove lagoon is home to a combination of turtles, sharks, and Galápagos penguins (the world's northernmost species), and the offshore Mariela rocks, crowded with seabirds; Urbina Bay (Bahía Urvina), where a violent uplift of the ocean floor in the 1950s left corals stranded on land; and Tagus cove, another area of lava fields.

Across the channel lies the outermost island of **Fernandina**, the most active volcanic island, where Punta Espinoza has good snorkeling, a massive marine iguana colony, and flightless cormorants.

Crossing the Equator

Of three islands north of the equator, only **Genovesa** (Tower) can be visited. Genovesa is home to Galápagos' only major colony of red-footed boobies, and also has great snorkeling, with warmer water and some fish species not seen elsewhere.

Returning south, the largest uninhabited island is **San Salvador** (Santiago or James), whose main visitor site is on the west coast at Puerto Egas. Here, besides the usual species, you can see the Galápagos fur seal. American oystercatchers are common here, and Sally Lightfoot crabs very abundant. This is also a highly varied snorkeling environment.

On the east shore of San Salvador lies Sullivan Bay (Bahía Sullivan), an area with a huge and recent lava field, where you can observe the pioneering recolonization of barren terrain by cactus and succulents. Across the bay lies **Bartolomé** island, with a climb through a blasted landscape of volcanic spatter cones to a high lookout point and a fabulous panoramic view of San Salvador to the west, Sombrero Chino island to the south, and nearby Pinnacle Rock. There is great swimming and snorkeling nearby, with penguins

common on the north beach of the island, and reef sharks and sometimes nesting turtles to be seen a short walk away on the south beach.

South of San Salvador, **Rábida** (Jervis) is an island of intense red sand, with a fine view from the nearby peak, and a lagoon where flamingoes feed and pelicans breed. The swimming and snorkeling are very good. **Caleta Tortuga Negra** on the north shore of Santa Cruz is a mangrove-lined inlet frequented by sharks, spotted-eagle and golden rays, and turtles.

17. SANTA CRUZ AND PUERTO AYORA *(see map p68)*

Santa Cruz and its port, Puerto Ayora, is the center of tourism in Galá-pagos, a large island with a sizeable population and plentiful attractions.

See page 68 for travel information. ATMs in Puerto Ayora do not give cash for many foreign bank cards, so bring cash, travelers' checks, or a credit card (note surcharges of up to 10 percent apply on credit-card payments).

A land-based visit, taking day trips to nearby islands, is about the cheapest way to see Galápagos, although you will miss some of the most interesting spots and spend a lot of time sailing. Some hotels *(see page 94)* offer complete programs of day tours, which can be quite luxurious.

Another option, for those on a budget with time to spare, is to fly to Baltra, then bus to Puerto Ayora and stay in a hotel while seeking fellow travelers and a suitable boat. Then relax, explore the island's possibilities, and enjoy the laid-back atmosphere of the port while waiting for your cruise to begin. This works best in the off season (Mar–May and Oct–Nov); in peak season (Dec–Jan and July–Aug) you could be stuck for weeks without a boat.

Above: sea kayaking in Elizabeth Bay
Left: giant tortoise

To avoid the hassle of seeking out individual boat captains, the recommended Moonrise Travel (Avenida Charles Darwin, opposite Banco Pacifico, tel: 252-6403) can arrange things for a little extra.

All cruises stop in Puerto Ayora at some point, loading up with supplies while passengers visit the unmissable **Darwin Research Station** (Mon–Fri 7am–5pm) to see the giant tortoises, including 'Lonesome George,' last survivor of the doomed Pinta Island species, observe the breeding program, visit the museum, and learn more about the island ecology.

Fun in the Ocean

With the abundance and variety of marine life and the unpredicability of the experience, scuba diving is very popular here. Few sites are for beginners, though. Scuba Iguana (Hotel Galápagos, tel: 252-6497, www.scuba iguana.com) by the Darwin Research Station, offers one- and two-day outings. Nauti Diving (Avenida Charles Darwin, tel: 252-6096, www.nautidiving. com), also offers eight- and ten-day dive tours (book in advance) of the most spectacular sites.

Puerto Ayora has good swimming and surfing beaches nearby, and surfboards and wetsuits can be rented at the Galápagos Tours Center on Avenida Baltra. Beautiful **Tortuga Bay** (Bahía Tortuga) is a one-hour walk west of town on a marked trail. Register at the gate (daily 6am–6.30pm), take food and water, and beware of a very strong undertow. A water taxi will take you across Academy Bay (Bahía Academy) to visit **Playa los Alemanes** for more advanced surfing, or the delightful nearby

swimming hole of Las Grietas. Out to the east is Garrapatero, another beautiful beach, which can be reached by road and has good wildlife viewing.

Trips to the humid **highlands**, known as the *scalesia* zone, are offered by local agencies, or you could hire a pick-up or use local transportation. Attractions here include visiting lava tubes (tunnels left by cooling lava) near the village of **Bellavista**, taking a look at **Los Gemelos**, a pair of huge sinkholes near the village of Santa Rosa (bus to Santa Rosa, 30-minutes, then walk), and hiking to see giant tortoises in the wild at the **El Chato Tortoise Reserve** (guide required).

Nightlife, mostly on the waterfront, is fun, and Wednesday nights, when many boat crews hit town, are liveliest. La Panga and Limón y Café are the best-known spots. La Taberna del Duende often has live Ecuadorean folk music. Of many small restaurants in town, there's excellent food at La Garrapata ($$) and Angermeyer Point (tel: 252-6452; $$) at Punta Estrada, a great spot overlooking Academy Bay; take a water taxi from the quay.

Right: sea lion swimming off the north coast of Isla San Salvador

Leisure Activities

SHOPPING

Ecuador is a cornucopia of hand-made goods, and few people will leave here without making some purchase of colorful and intricate local handicrafts. Prices are low by US or European standards, and bargaining is possible – even expected – in most places, including all but the high-end stores. Be fair, though; merciless bargaining is unreasonable, when you consider how low the wage of the average person is. And don't expect a discount on credit-card purchases – local banks take a huge cut.

The pre-hispanic peoples of the Andes were remarkably fixated on the production of textiles, assigning great value and importance to the weaver's skill. This tradition has survived and, in fact, thrived in modern Ecuador, with some low-tech mechanical innovations in some areas – such as the use of treadle looms to replace the ancient back-strap loom in the making of some, but not all, textile items. Woven goods still make up the majority of handicrafts available in Ecuador, and pieces range from wall-hangings, blankets, scarves, hats, bags, ponchos, shawls, cushion covers, belts and baskets, and, of course, Panama hats (which originated here, and were exported to Panama retailers). The materials used range from sheep's wool and cotton, through sisal fiber from the common agave plant, palm fronds, and leather. Ecuador does not yet produce much alpaca wool, although attempts are being made to introduce it; these items are imported from Peru and Bolivia.

Other crafts, such as jewelry, carvings in wood and *tagua* ('vegetable ivory'), leatherwork, bread-dough ornaments and ceramics are practiced in a variety of local styles in many different parts of the country.

Do not purchase anything made from black coral, a once-common marine species, now seriously endangered because of excessive collecting for the manufacture of jewelry.

Avoid anything made with wildlife products, such as macaw feathers and animal skins. It is illegal to export them from Ecuador or take them into your country – and with good reason, since so many species have been driven to the verge of extinction by this trade.

Quito

Everything produced in Ecuador can be found somewhere in Quito, though at higher prices than in the place of origin. In fact, most of the top-quality handicrafts are made exclusively either for exporters or high-end handicraft stores in Quito. So if that is what you seek, and price is not a problem, the place to find it is Quito.

Starting at the top, **Folklore** (Avenida Colón E10–53 y Caamaño, tel: 256-3085; also in the Hotel Hilton Colón, Patria y Amazonas; www. olgafisch.com) offers a big selection of truly elegant handicrafts, along with a private museum of folk and pre-hispanic art. The main competitor at this level is **Galería Latina** (Juan León Mera N23–69, tel: 254-0380; www.galerialatina-quito.com), a big store, with high-quality handicrafts of all descriptions, including items from Peru and Bolivia. **La Bodega/Ag Joyería** (Juan Leon Mera N22–24, tel: 255-0276) has slightly lower prices, and also offers antiques and silver jewelry. **Casa Verde** (Juan León Mera 404–A y Robles, tel: 255-1796) sells antiques and quality gift items, while **Plaza Naya** (Juan León Mera y

Left: poultry deals at Saquilisí market
Right: mini-stall made from dough

Roca, tel: 222-1841; www.getandgo.org) carries a range of fashion handicrafts. For a big range of mid- to low-end crafts, go to the **Centro Artesanal** (Juan León Mera) and **Reina Victoria** (Jorge Washington), which features scores of kiosks and vendors peddling every craft you can imagine. To view, and perhaps buy, the work of hopeful local artists, **Parque El Ejido** hosts a large open-air art gallery every Saturday.

If you need to do some food shopping, you'll find a good range of groceries at the excellent **Supermaxi** supermarket and its big brother, **Megamaxi**, which are located all over the city. There's a well-stocked Megamaxi at Avenida 6 de Diciembre y J. Moreno and the Ecovía goes right by it. In the same vein, an excellent delicatessen in the Mariscal district is **El Español** (Juan León Mera 863 y Wilson). A one-stop shopping spot for most of the everyday necessities that you might have lost or left behind is the **Espiral Centro Comercial**, just a block away from the Centro Artesanal at Amazonas y Jorge Washington.

Ecuador produces top-quality cigars *(cigarros)*, the best and biggest of which retail for about $5 apiece. There are cigar stores in the big hotels, and there's one at the Quicentro shopping center, Shyris y Naciones Unidas.

Otavalo

Otavalo is *the* market center of Ecuador for handicraft shopping, with big market days on Saturday and Wednesday, and something happening every day of the week. In addition to the packed area of market vendors on the Plaza de Ponchos, there are numerous handicraft stores on the streets of Jaramillo, Bolivar and Sucre, for several blocks on either side of the market; literally, a shopper's feast.

In the surrounding villages, **Peguche** and **Agato** are home to the handicraft workshops of **José Cotacachi** and **Miguel Andrango** (Tahuantinsuyu), two of the best-known weavers of the region. Here you go directly to the source, and can see weavings being made and take photos.

Cotacachi

This is the leather-goods center of Ecuador, with dozens of stores lining the town's main street. The leather itself is generally of excellent quality, though the finish can be variable. Before you buy, thoroughly check the stitching, buttonholes, zippers, and buckles – all the nitpicky details that make such a difference.

San Antonio de Ibarra

The wood-carving capital of the highlands (not to be confused with Ibarra), San Antonio de Ibarra is located just off the Pan-American highway before it reaches Ibarra, about a 30-minute drive north of Otavalo. Just about everyone in town makes woodcarvings, mostly in a local Mannerist style, although you will find a few that are more original.

Salasaca, Pelileo, and Baños

On the road to Baños, the town of Salasaca is the center of an ethnic group believed to have been originally transported here by the Incas from Bolivia. They traditionally wear black ponchos and white, broad-brimmed hats, and weave woolen tapestries, which are sold in the town.

Pelileo, 5km (3 miles) toward Baños, is an entire village full of stores and factories that are dedicated to making blue jeans; you can buy a good pair of denims here at a very good price.

Left: shopping for handicrafts on the station platform at Guamote

In Baños, the local specialty is *melcocha*, a very chewy, sweet, and sticky toffee, not recommended for anyone with dental problems. You can buy it at market stands near the bus station, where they also sell bundles of sugar cane. Besides a national range of crafts, many stores carry painted balsa-wood figurines representing animals and especially parrots and macaws, which are a specialty of the region.

Riobamba

The small town of Guano, 8km (5 miles) from Riobamba, specializes in hand-made carpets and rugs. There are a number of workshops along the roadside as you arrive in the town that will make a rug or carpet to order for you.

Cañar

In this cold highland town superb hand-woven cotton belts are made, and some of the best are produced by prisoners incarcerated in the local jail. You can buy them at the jail (Colón y 3 de Noviembre), which is a fascinating experience in itself; just state your mission, and ask the guards to let you in (and out!). Cañar also has an interesting market on Sundays, with a number of handicrafts stands.

Cuenca

The Cuenca region is the source of a variety of handicrafts. *Ikat* (weaving with tie-dyed thread) is a specialty of the area around Gualaceo some 25km (15½ miles) southeast of Cuenca, while Chordeleg, 4km (2½ miles) farther south, is a center for ceramics and gold and silver filigree jewelry. Both of these villages have craft stands and stores. A short taxi ride from Gualaceo, the villages of Bulzhun and Bulcay are centers of *ikat* weaving production.

In Cuenca itself, **Arte Artesanías y Antigüedades** at Borrero y Córdova, is a top-end handicraft collection. On the next block, between Sucre and Córdova, **El Tucán** is also recommended. This area has a number of other craft stores, including the gift shop within the **Museo de las Culturas Aborígenes**, Larga y Hermano Miguel. Here you'll find a good selection of top-quality handicrafts as well as replicas of local antiquities. Fine locally made candles are sold at **Candere** (Córdova 5–72 y Hermano Miguel).

Functional domestic ceramics, thrown by potters with workshops in the area, are on display at **Artesa** (Cordero 984 y Gran Colombia), while more artistic creations can be seen at the gallery of **Eduardo Vega**, near the viewpoint of El Turi.

Cuenca is a center of the famous Panama hat industry, and you can see them being made at **Homero Ortega** (Gil Ramírez Dávalos 386, tel: 280-9000), near the bus station. The company offers factory tours (weekdays 9am–noon, 3–6pm) and has a shop. Closer to the center of the city, **Sombreros Barranco** (Calle Larga 10–41 y Torres) also makes and sells hats, and has a hat museum.

Above: Otavalan women selling handicrafts in the old town at Quito

EATING OUT

With almost every fruit, spice, and vegetable known to gastronomy growing on its territory, Ecuador has developed a splendid variety of cooking styles and dishes. Regional cuisines vary from Pacific through Andes to Oriente, with celebrated local styles in Cuenca, Quito, and Esmeraldas.

When eating in the Oriente, cassava, plantain, and rice leap to the top of the menu, along with a variety of local river catfish *(bagre)* and perhaps even *piraña*, which are tasty, if a bit bony. Highland cooking is known as hearty food, heavy on potatoes, grains, cheese, and meat, especially pork. Soups, always on traditional menus, ward off the highland chill and perhaps counter dehydration at high altitude.

A famous national dish is *locro*, a potato, cheese, and grain-based soup, with vegetables and sometimes chicken, pork, beef, or egg. If you find what look like tiny germinated seeds in your soup, it has been made with *quinoa*, a very nutritious Andean grain. *Llapingachos*, fried patties of cheese, onion, and potato, are a popular snack or side dish, as are *empanadas* – miniature fried pastries, stuffed with meat *(de morocho)*, plantain *(verdes)*, corn *(de maíz)*, or cheese *(queso)*. Throughout the country there is a Cantonese-derived cuisine known as *chifa*.

Starchy Staples

The ancient Andean peoples considered corn a sacred plant, and it has not lost its appeal. It's usually a sweet, juicy variety with large kernels and a unique flavor. Corn on the cob *(choclo)*, toasted corn *(camcha)*, pocorn *(cangil)*, and boiled kernels *(mote)* accompany or are part of the majority of dishes. Ground corn is the main ingredient of *humitas* (boiled corn patties) both sweet and savory, and corn husks make the wrapper. And there is *mote pillo*, a corn patty, fried with egg and cheese. Germinated, boiled, and fermented corn becomes *chicha de jora*, a home-brew beer, and purple corn is used to make non-alcoholic *chicha morada*.

Other popular starchy staples are cassava *(yuca)*, sweet potatoes *(camote)* and, of course, rice *(arroz)*, which accompanies a multitude of dishes throughout the country.

Meat and Seafood

Meat is plentiful, but if you are offered wild game, refuse it on ecological grounds. Typically, beef *(carne de res)* is served as steak: the standard *bistec* or thick juicy *lomo*. Small chunks grilled on a skewer are known as *anticuchos*. Lamb *(cordero)*, sucking pig *(lechón)*, pork *(chancho)*, sausage *(salchicha* or *chorizo)*, ham *(jamón)*, and bacon *(tocino)* are all common on the sierra menu. Pork is usually served roasted *(asado)* or deep fried *(fritada)*. If you're really adventurous, try guinea pig *(cuy)* – really quite tasty.

The Pacific Ocean supplies endless choices of seafood. *Ceviche* (raw seafood marinated in lime juice) is popular, and best eaten in a fishing port for absolute freshness – shrimp and crayfish *(langostinos* and *camarones)* are an exception, since they are always cooked. Sea bass *(corvina),* mahi mahi *(dorado),* tuna *(atún)*, snapper *(pargo),* mackerel *(sierra),* and swordfish *(pez espada)* are the prime fish, while every imaginable clam *(almeja)*, oyster *(ostión),* crab *(cangrejo),* squid *(calamar),* or octopus *(pulpo)* – collectively known as *mariscos* – will arrive on your plate when you order anything featuring the word *mixto*. Lobster *(langosta)* is overfished and endangered here, so resist the temptation.

The Esmeraldas region prepares fish with a special local twist, cooking it in coconut milk, in a style known as *encocado*.

What to Drink

The main local alcoholic drink worth sampling is beer – local brands are Pilsen and Club, both pretty good lagers. Ecuador has a way to go before it produces a wine worth drinking, so Argentine, Chilean, and Peruvian wines are the affordable (not cheap) option. *Chicha,* Andean corn beer, is always home-made, usually with questionable hygiene; thousands of years of history are behind this sour, but not unpleasant brew, and it's quite nutritious. On cold highland nights, people tend to offer *hervidas* – hot drinks made of raw, fiery rum *(trago)* and sweetened fruit juice; a cooler option is the *canelazo*, with cinnamon, sugar, and lime.

Fruit juices are a delicious treat, if you can be sure they are made with boiled or bottled water. Some of the superb fruits that

---

Right: El Nispero restaurant in Quito, serving typical Ecuadorean food

you almost certainly will not have tasted at home are tree tomato *(tomate de árbol),* cape gooseberry *(uvilla),* custard apple *(chirimoya),* and naranjilla.

Where to Eat

Big cities, especially Quito, have a great range of international restaurants, with Italian, Middle Eastern, Indian, Chinese, and French being the most prominent, plus, of course, the usual multinational fast-food outlets.

Most mid-level and lower-priced restaurants serve a fixed-price lunch, and sometimes dinner too, which is substantially less expensive than choosing from the a la carte menu. In the restaurants listed below, the approximate cost of an a la carte meal for one without drinks is:

$$$ = more than $15
$$ = $5–15
$ = under $5

Quito

Theatrum
Manabí y Guayaqui, in Teatro Sucre, 2nd floor (old city)
Tel: 257-1011
Excellent Ecuadorean and international cuisine and an opulent atmosphere at Quito's oldest theatre. $$$

El Galpón
Colón E10–53 y Caamaño
Tel: 254-6961
Gourmet Ecuadorean cuisine in a museum atmosphere, with objects from the adjacent Olga Fisch Folk Museum. Recommended. $$$

Sake
Paul Rivet N30–166 y Whymper
Tel: 252-4818
Japanese food here is expensive, very trendy, and superb. $$$

La Cueva del Oso
Chile 1046 y Venezuela (old city)
Tel: 257-2786
Elegant, low-key Art Deco surroundings and good Ecuadorean cuisine. Not overly expensive. $$$

Trattoria Sole y Luna
Whymper N31–29 y Coruña
Tel: 223-5865
Classy Italian restaurant. $$$

El Níspero
Valladolid N24–438 y Cordero
Tel: 222-6398
Very good local cuisine. $$$

El Pajonal
Homero Salas y Altar
Tel: 244-9816
Right by the airport. Good place for a last meal in Ecuador. Typical Ecuadorean food, mainly meat. Live music Friday nights. $$

Pekin Restaurant
Whymper N28–42 y Orellana
Tel: 223-5273
Pretty good Chinese food. $$

La Casa de Mi Abuela
Juan León Mera 1649
Tel: 256-5667
Limited selection of good steaks, at a reasonable price. Nothing for vegetarians. $$

Le Arcate
Baquedano 358 y Juan León Mera
Tel: 223-7659
Good thin-crust pizza. $$

Mango Tree Café
Foch E43–10 y Amazonas
Good breakfast place (yoghurt, granola, etc).
Lunch has pasta and vegetarian choices. $$

Este Café
Juan León Mera N23–54 y Wilson
Tel: 254-2488
Good, friendly breakfast spot, with English-
language books and magazines. $$

Café Galletti
Carrión E5–40 y Reina Victoria
Tel: 252-7361
Gourmet Ecuador-grown coffee and good
cakes and pastries. Recommended. $$

Crepes & Waffles
*Orellana y Juan León Mera (near Hotel
Marriott)*
Serves exactly that. $$

El Arabe
Reina Victoria 627 y Carrión
Tel: 254-9414
Great lamb dishes, very good value. $

S'panes
*Amazonas 261 y Jorge Washington/Eloy
Alfaro y Portugal*
Tel: 256-2930
Colombian-style fast-food chain, with tasty,
filling food. Try the *arepas con chorizo* (spicy
sausage corn tortillas) or *caribañolas*. $

Sakti
Carrión 641 y Amazonas
Tel: 252-0466
Indian vegetarian restaurant. $

Otavalo
Ali Shungu
Calle Quito y Miguel Egas
Tel: 292-0750
Original and tasty international menu of
vegetarian and meat dishes. Bar and good
wine list. Highly recommended. $$

Quino
Roca y García Moreno
Seafood. Recommended at weekends
when the fish is freshest. $$

Mi Otavalito
Sucre y Colón
Good Ecuadorean meat and fish dishes.
Local feel, traditional décor. $$

Pizza Siciliana
Morales at Sucre
Popular, comfortable atmosphere to sit
around, write postcards, and drink beer. $$

El Indio
Sucre y Salinas
Fried chicken and typical local food.
Always busy; good value. $

Baños
Quilombo
Montalvo y 12 de Noviembre
Tel: 274-2880
Argentine steak extravaganza, served in
generous portions. $$

Cuisine de Provence,
Halflants y Rocafuerte
Tel: 274-0911
Good, simple French cuisine. Excellent value. Recommended. **$$**

Mama Inés
Ambato y Halflants
Tel: 274-0538
Popular sidewalk café. Good family food. **$$**

Café Rico Pan
Ambato y Maldonado
Tel: 274-0387
Good breakfasts, pizzas, and full meals. **$$**

Café Ali Cumba
Maldonado y Ambato
Tel: 274-1385
Small café; good pastries and coffee. **$**

Pancho Villa
Montalvo y 16 de Diciembre, opposite park
Good Mexican food; inexpensive. **$**

Riobamba

El Delirio
Corner Primera Constituyente/Rocafuerte
Tel: 296-6441
Historic building, a bit touristy, but nice atmosphere and food. **$$**

Cabaña Montecarlo
Garcia Moreno 21–40 y 10 de Agosto
Tel: 296-2844
Hearty international and local food. **$$**

El Fogón del Puente
Daniel León Borja/ y Duchicela
Tel: 296-9751
International food; good meat dishes. **$$**

Gran Havana
Daniel León Borja 42–52 y Duchicela
Tel: 296-8088
Filling good-value Cuban food. **$**

Cuenca

Inti-Sumag
Gran Colombia 787 y Luis Cordero
Tel: 283-1390
In Hotel El Dorado, with great views and excellent food. Recommended. **$$$**

El Jordán
Larga 6–111 y Borrero
Tel: 285-0517
Sumptuous, faux-Arabian *fin-de-siécle* style, with objects for sale. Arab and international cuisine. Low-price fixed lunch. **$$**

El Maíz
Larga 1–279 y Los Molinos
Tel: 284-0224
Cuenca-style cuisine, great for lunch. **$$**

Molinos del Batán
12 de Abril y Puente Centenario
Tel: 281-1531
Good Ecuadorcan food on the riverbank. **$$**

Raymipampa
Benigno Malo 8–59, on Parque Calderón
Tel: 283-1459
Nice, family-type restaurant in a great location. Very popular with local people. **$$**

Il Cavalino
Benigno Malo 6–91 y Córdova
Tel: 284-3845
Pizza and pasta. **$$**

Aguacolla Café
Todos Santos, on the steps to Puente Roto
Tel: 282-4029
Wholefood/organic café. Live music. **$$**

Café Austria
Corner of Benigno Malo and Jarmaillo
Tel: 284-0899
Good coffee, sandwiches, and pastries. **$$**

Puerto López

Spondylus
Malecón Izurieta
Good seafood. Slow service, but popular. **$$**

Bella Italia
Monatalvo y Abdón Calderón
Great Italian food, good service. **$$**

Whale Café
Malecón Izurieta, south end
Sandwiches, meals, pizza, and – a rare treat – salads that are safe to eat. English menu, books, and ambience. **$$**

Left: a dish of local trout at El Maíz restaurant, Cuenca

NIGHTLIFE

The party habits of travelers are well satisfied in the teeming bars, discos, and *peñas* (folk-music clubs) of the major Ecuadorean cities. Local music is a mix of Latin and indigenous styles, some with roots deep in the Andes, others imported from Spain, Africa, and the Caribbean.

Highland bands play haunting music of pentatonic scales, using reed flutes *(quena)* and pan pipes *(zampoña* or *rondador)*, with *charango* (like a mandolin), harp, guitar, bass drum, and an assortment of percussion. On the coast *salsa*, *cumbia*, and *merengue* fill the humid air. *Marimba*, based on the xylophone-like instrument, is dominant in Esmeraldas province, though it is mostly local folk and family music. Rock, hip-hop, trance, and other Euro-American music is heard in discos and on radios everywhere.

Some places charge a cover, some have a minimum consumption charge, and some charge an entrance which includes one drink. Sunday through Tuesday is pretty dead in most places. Recent municipal ordinances in Quito require night spots and bars to close at 2am, though in any Latin country such a law is doomed to be flouted.

The newspapers *El Comercio* (www. elcomercio.com) in Quito, *El Universo* (www.eluniverso.com) in Guayaquil, and *El Mercurio* (www.elmercurio.com.ec) in Cuenca, have entertainment listings.

Quito
Café-Bars
Bogarín
Reina Victoria N24–217 y Lizardo García
Tel: 255-5057
Pizza and live music.

El Pobre Diablo
Isabel la Católica y Madrid
Jazz and snacks. Civilized.

La Boca del Lobo
Calama 284 y Reina Victoria
Tel: 223-4083
Wine bar; good place to chat and meet.

Varadero
Reina Victoria y La Pinta
Restaurant. Live Cuban music Thursdays.

Discos
Blues Bar
República 476 y Almagro
Tel: 222-3206
Basement bar for classic rock fans.

Bunga
Francisco Salazar y 12 de Octubre
Young Quito crowd. New-wave Spanish rock and local bands. No sign outside.

Elysium
García Moreno N6–22 y Mejía
Big and very hip Studio 54-type revival.

Peñas
Ñucanchi Huasi
Avenida Universitaria 496 y Armero
Tel: 254-0967
Long-established folk-music club.
Tues–Sat.

Pubs
Reina Victoria Pub
Reina Victoria 530 y Roca
Tel: 222-6369
English-style, with imported ales and Scotch.

Turtle's Head Bar
La Niña 626 y Juan León Mera
Tel: 256-5544
Microbrewery, with food, darts, pool, and a gruff Scottish owner.

Above: Hallowe'en night at the Elysium nightclub, Quito
Right: a quiet night in Puerto López

Salsoteca
Seseribó
Veintimilla y 12 de Octubre
Tel: 256-3598
Classic salsa spot.

Otavalo

Otavalo is a center for Andean traditional music, with many music stores in town.

Discos
Habana Club
Quito y 31 de Octubre
A popular club where local young people hang out.

Peñas
Peña Jampa
Calle Jaramillo y Quiroga
Young crowd, Latin and folk music, and raucous dancing.

Peña da Pinto
Calle Colón between Sucre and Bolivar
Beautifully decorated and spacious place serving cocktails and snacks.

Baños

A cluster of bars on Eloy Alfaro is the nightlife center of town.

Bars
Hard Rock Café
Eloy Alfaro y Ambato
Traveler's hangout, no relation to the original. Good cocktails.

Peñas
Peña Ananitay
6 de Diciembre y Espejo
Popular venue for live traditional folk music and dancing.

Salsa Dancing
Bamboos Bar
Eloy Alfaro y Oriente
Dancing, live music at weekends.

Puerto López

Bars
Magic Night
South end of Malecón Izurieta
Excellent cocktails; friendly.

La Resaca
On the beach, opposite Malecón Izurieta
A converted fishing boat; great atmosphere.

Cuenca

Café-Bars
Kaos
Honorato Vásquez 6–11 y Hermano Miguel
Popular local bar. Italian food. Pool table.

Eucalyptus
Gran Colombia 9–41 y Padre Aguirre
Tel: 284-9157
International café and pub. Popular with travelers. Opens early, closes late.

Tapas y Canciones
Calle Larga 6–111 y Borrero
Tel: 285-0092
Very traditional café, with live Latin music.

Disco
La Fábrica
Huayna Capac y Juan Jaramillo
Popular local party spot.

Salsa Dancing
La Mesa Salsoteca
Gran Colombia 335 y Tomás Ordóñez
Tel: 283-3300
Local salsadrome. Big, brassy and crowded.

CALENDAR OF EVENTS

Ecuador celebrates a large number of regional and local *fiestas* (festivals) throughout the year. A few are worthy of scheduling your visit specifically so you can join in the celebrations, and most are fun if you just happen to be there. Numerous civic festivals commemorate the founding or anniversary of a town, or some Independence event, but the majority – and usually the most interesting – are religious festivals. These blend indigenous culture and Christian customs, and, as a result, they are often colorful and intriguing.

Most festivals involve a lot of drinking, which can sometimes create difficult situations. People want you to drink with them, and they usually don't want you to leave. Unless you really want to stay and get drunk, accept no more than a drink or two, then move on. The big public festivals are good for photography, but watch your camera, and be very sensitive to people's attitudes in small villages. They may object to you taking pictures, so if there seems to be a problem, stop snapping right away.

Accommodations fill up quickly for major festivals, so be sure you have a properly confirmed reservation at those times. During Easter week, beach resorts are particularly crowded.

January

January 6. Festival of the Magi (Epiphany) with parades and Christmas carols. Ambato, Riobamba, Pujilí, Cuenca, and other places

February/March

February or March. Carnival. A moveable feast preceded by a week or two of heavy water-throwing in the streets, climaxing in celebrations from the Sunday through Tuesday before Ash Wednesday. Nationwide, but most congenial in Ambato, where they hold parades and throw flowers instead of water.

March

March 4. Gualaceo (Peach Festival). Fruit and flower parades, and floats in the river.

March or April. Easter Week. A moveable feast, from Palm Sunday (palm-frond crosses and ornaments) through the following Easter Sunday. Nationwide. Quito has a famous Good Friday procession of cross-bearing penitents. Throughout the week people eat *fanesca*, a stew made of dried cod and grains.

March 21/22. Mitad del Mundo (Equinox). Not a festival exactly. Nevertheless, the monument area gets extremely lively with people celebrating the sun's zenith passage over the equator.

Above: musicians performing in the Plaza San Francisco, Quito

April

April 21. Independence. Commemorating the independence Battle of Tapi, Riobamba celebrates for several days with bullfights, dancing, and parades.

May

May 18. Mindo Town Anniversary. Parties, sports, parades.

May 24. Battle of Pichincha. A major national holiday, with military parades, partying, and drinking. Nationwide.

May/June. Corpus Christi (Thursday after Trinity Sunday). Pujilí: masked and costumed dancers and intrepid climbs to retrieve prizes tied to a tall pole. Cuenca: fireworks and paper hot-air balloons in the main square. Worth going out of your way for.

June

June 21–29. Los San Juanes. A series of festivals starting with the pre-Hispanic Inti Raymi (winter solstice) festival (21st), and merging into St John the Baptist (24th), and SS Peter & Paul (29th). Dancing in the streets, exotic costumes, ritual battles (quite dangerous), with bonfires on the night of the 29th, which those women who wish to get pregnant have to jump across. Entertaining. Otavalo and other villages throughout the area.

July

July 16. Virgin of Carmen, A Christian/indigenous shrine with fair and pilgrimage. Chambo, near Riobamba.

July 24/25. Simón Bolivar/Guayaquil Founding Day. Civic festival with cultural events and parades. Guayaquil.

August

August 5. Foundation Day, Esmeraldas, and **August 6–10**. Anniversary Festival, San Lorenzo. Both of these festivals offer a good chance to hear *marimba* music and sample Afro-Ecuadorean culture at its most festive.

August 10. First declaration of Independence, with cultural events throughout the month. Quito.

September

September 2–15. Yamor. A mainly *mestizo* festival, featuring swimming and reed boat races on Laguna San Pablo; bullfights, cockfights, folk dances. Otavalo, Cotacachi,

September 6. Virgin of the Swan. Annual religious parade. Mindo.

September 21/22. Mitad del Mundo (Equinox). Second equinox of the year.

September 23/24. Mama Negra. Feast of the dark virgin. Masked, costumed dances, representing black slaves. Latacunga.

October

All Month. Celebrations to honor the Virgin of the Holy Water. Baños.

October 9. Independence. Parades and dancing in the streets. Guayaquil.

October 12. Festival de la Balsa Manteña. People dressed as ancient Manteño sailors build and launch balsa rafts. Salango.

October 29–31. Mojandas Arriba. A walk from Quito to Otavalo via Lagunas de Mojanda, with celebrations in Otavalo.

November

November 2. Day of the Dead. Feasting and offerings for the recently dead in private homes; festive gatherings in cemeteries. Nationwide.

November 3. Independence. Parades, fireworks, parties. Cuenca.

December

December 6. Founding of Quito. Bullfights, parties, parades.

December 15/16. Baños Anniversary. Street parties and bands.

December 24. Christmas Eve. Morning Parade of the Christ child. Cuenca.

December 31. New Year's Eve. Burning of effigies representing the old year. Satirical and lively. Nationwide.

Practical
Information

GETTING THERE

By Air

The following airlines offer non-stop flights to Quito: American, TACA and LANChile from Miami; Continental from Houston; KLM from Amsterdam; Iberia and Air Europa from Madrid; TACA and LANChile from Lima; Avianca from Bogotá; Copa from Panama.

Quito airport is conveniently located about 15 minutes from the city center, though a new one is being built farther away. A taxi ride to the center is currently about $5.

By Road

From Peru: at the Zarumilla/Huaqillas crossing on the main coastal Pan-American highway; at Macará/Sullana, a quiet spot favored by those wishing to avoid the chaos and hassle of the Pan-American; between Zumba and San Ignacio, south of Vilcabamba, a remote but increasingly popular route, connecting to the interesting Chachapoyas region of northern Peru.

From Colombia: at Tulcán/Ipiales. Note that road travel in Colombia is considered unsafe.

Ormeño Internacional (in Quito: Shyris y Portugál, tel: 246-0027), runs an international bus from Lima to Quito.

TRAVEL ESSENTIALS

When to Visit

Ecuador's seasonal variations are wildly eccentric, as befits a country with a huge altitude range located on the equator. The highlands claim two three-month rainy seasons beginning around the equinoxes, in March and September, and two dry seasons the rest of the year. Highland seasonal temperatures do not vary much.

The Oriente (eastern tropical lowlands) is always hot and can be rainy anytime, but especially from May through September.

The coast has, broadly speaking, both a southern climate and a northern climate, the divide occurring somewhere north of Manta. The south coast, including the Galápagos, has cool, cloudy weather, with occasional drizzly rain May through September, while the rest of the year is warm and sunny. The north coast has the opposite climate, with sun during May through September, and sporadic rain and cloud the rest of the year. These are just the general outlines, and some areas have variant local climates.

All this means that in Ecuador the sun is always shining somewhere, it's always raining somewhere, and there's always something you can do somewhere.

Visas and Passports

Your passport must be valid for at least six months on entering the country. You have to fill in an immigration slip, which you surrender on leaving the country. Immigration will allow most nationalities up to 90 days in the country upon entry, so ask for this period when you enter. If you stay longer, you can extend for 30 days at a time, to a maximum of 180 days total. Go to the Dirección Nacional de Migraciones (Isla Seymour 44–174 y Río Cocatel, tel: 224-7510) in Quito. Visas are not required for the countries whose consulates are listed on page 99.

The law requires you to carry your passport with you at all times during your stay. A

Left: tourists riding on the roof of a train **Right:** ranchero-style bus

photocopy is not, strictly speaking, acceptable – but one legalized by a public notary will pass muster with most officials.

Customs

Foreign tourists have few problems with customs when carrying items for personal use, such as climbing gear or a laptop. Large items obviously not for travel use may carry a substantial duty.

Vaccinations

Inoculations against typhoid, tetanus, hepatitis A and B, and rabies are recommended, plus yellow fever and malaria prophylaxis for visitors heading for lowland areas of the north coast or Oriente.

Dress

Formal clothes are rarely needed. Although Ecuadoreans may dress up for eating out, even most expensive restaurants are resigned to the casual dress of foreign tourists.

When traveling around Ecuador, be prepared for all kinds of weather extremes. The highland parks experience sub-freezing weather at night, while highland valleys have a mild, pleasant climate. The coast and Oriente can be hot. Climbing, of course, requires specialized gear, which you can rent. Raingear, a hat, and swimwear are essential, as are good walking shoes or hiking boots.

Useful Items

Travelers should bring a flashlight, batteries, a pocket knife, toilet paper, a lightweight towel, a universal bathroom drain-plug, and a money/passport pouch (worn *inside* your clothes). High-factor sunblock and insect repellent are essential. An inflatable travel pillow, eye-mask, and ear-plugs are very useful for bus rides and other situations where you otherwise could not sleep. Lightweight binoculars are very good to have.

Time

Ecuador has two time zones. The mainland is GMT minus 5 hours, and Galápagos is GMT minus 6 hours.

Electricity

The current is 110V, 60 Hz. Most power points take US-style flat-prong plugs.

GETTING ACQUAINTED

Note that in this book, 'Ecuador' and 'Ecuadorean' refers to this region of the Andes and its inhabitants throughout its history, although the Republic of Ecuador was not so named until 1830.

Geography

Despite its relatively modest land area of 283,561sq. km (109,483 sq. miles) – about the size of Italy – Ecuador is one of the world's 17 megadiverse nations. It packs so many environments and habitats into its varied equatorial geography that it is a magnet for natural scientists, birders, orchid fanciers, mountaineers and other specialists.

The Pacific coastal plain, running north-south parallel to the Andes, ranges from arid in the south to teeming rainforest in the north with cloudforest clinging to rugged slopes on both flanks of the Andes, and a vast sweep of lowland rainforest to the east.

Volcanoes, ranging from extinct through highly active and occasionally dangerous, dominate the north and central Andean highlands, topped by 6,310-m (20,696-ft) Chimborazo. The website www.epn.edu.ec has useful information on volcano status – when it's functioning. The southern mountains are lower, older, and more eroded. Between the western and eastern ranges lies an extended chain of highland valleys with benign, well watered climates, ideal for dairy and sheep farming, and agriculture.

Government and Economy

Ecuador's congress and president are democratically elected, and have been continuously since 1979, despite several constitutional crises. Presidential elections are held every four years. Voting is compulsory, from age 18 onward.

The economy is mainly privately owned, with state or military participation in some sectors, such as aviation. Oil is the largest foreign-exchange earner, though agriculture, flowers and fisheries are also important, and employ far more people. High oil and commodity prices are currently staving off severe unemployment, poverty, and social problems, which have destabilized governments in the recent past.

Right: outside a schoolhouse north of Quilotoa

practical information

Religion

Ecuador is about 90 percent Roman Catholic, and very actively so. Full freedom of religion exists, however, and evangelist sects, Mormons, and other groups are also highly visible. Indigenous people often combine their Christianity with ancient beliefs and rites – classic syncretism – especially in the Oriente. Visitors are welcome in churches during Mass, as long as they are quiet and respectful, and avoid flash photography.

Population

Prior to the Spanish invasion the population was divided along regional and ethnic lines, and these distinctions have survived among the Quichua-speaking highland Indians, and in the Oriente, where even the languages are different. The Spanish brought in a white ruling class, which remains influential. Subsequent racial mixing produced a largely *mestizo* (mixed Indian-European) nation: about 65 percent of a population of some 12.5 million today. On the coast, the importation of slaves created Afro-Ecuadorean groups, especially in the north. A sprinkling of other nationalities has immigrated throughout the republican era, including Chinese and a small but prominent Arab community.

How Not to Offend

Greeting acquaintances with a handshake is customary, and men often give women acquaintances a chaste kiss on the cheek. Everyone expects at least a "*buenos días*" before you start into business. Politeness is highly regarded, and all arguments should be subject to this rule. Don't shout at or abuse anyone, no matter what the provocation. This does not imply surrender – polite firmness and persistence can be very effective.

Hours and Holidays

As a rough guide, most businesses serving the general public open Monday to Friday 9am to 6pm, and Saturday 9am to 1pm. Shops are often open a bit later, and those catering to tourists sometimes open all day Saturday. Opening hours of government offices are generally Monday to Friday 9am to 5 or 6pm, closed noon–2pm. Banks are open Monday to Friday 9am–1.30pm and 2.30–6.30pm, and Saturday 9.30am–2pm.

If a public holiday falls mid-week, or on a Saturday or Sunday, it's usually moved to the nearest Friday or Monday to create a long weekend.

Public Holidays

January 1: New Year's Day
February/March (variable): Monday and Tuesday of Carnival
March/April (variable): Thursday and Friday of Easter week
May 1: Worker's Day
May 24: Battle of Pichincha
Late May: Corpus Christi (variable)
August 10: Independence Day
October 9: Independence of Guayaquil
November 2: All Souls Day
November 3: Independence of Cuenca
December 6: Foundation of Quito
December 25: Christmas

MONEY MATTERS

The official currency of Ecuador is the US dollar. Coins are a mixture of locally minted and American, the largest being a local brass one-dollar coin. Euros can easily be changed into dollars at reasonable exchange rates. *Casas de Cambio* are a better option for this than banks. A good exchange place in Quito is VazCorp, at Amazonas y Roca. They will also change travelers' checks into dollars for a 2 percent discount. Always carry sufficient cash when traveling to provincial areas away from big cities.

Credit Cards & Travelers' Checks

All major international credit cards are acceptable, but many businesses levy a surcharge of up to 10 percent on transactions made with them, and even when they don't, credit cards reduce your bargaining power for shopping. Travelers' checks are negotiable for a 2–4 percent discount.

There are plenty of ATMs, which usually charge a flat fee of $1–2 per transaction. In principle, this is the best way to travel, gathering cash as you need it. However, machines can be unpredictable, denying some international cash cards, and even arbitrarily confiscating them on occasion. Retrieving them can be a lengthy and difficult business, so carry a duplicate card. In Quito the Banco de Guayaquil machines are reliable, and will give up to $500 at one time. Note that ATMs in Ecuador will not show your bank balance, so you need internet access to your account to get that information. For security you should have a credit card, travelers' checks or some other option besides an ATM card.

Tax and Service

Prices at the better restaurants and hotels are usually quoted without tax and service charges, which, when factored in, will add 22 percent to the bill.

Tipping

It is usual to tip 10 percent or so for decent service in a restaurant. If they already include a service charge, tip 5 percent or so for good service. Taxi drivers do not expect tips, although if hiring a car for a long stretch, a tip for the driver would be a friendly gesture. Elsewhere, tipping is discretionary. Baggage handlers, tour bus drivers, and guides who give good service are also tipworthy. Tips are also recommended for Galápagos boat crews and for staff at lodges where service charges are not included in the price.

Airport Tax

International departure tax is $25 from Quito or Guayaquil. There's no tax payable on domestic flights.

GETTING AROUND

Quito is easily the most convenient base from which to travel around Ecuador, and most of the information below assumes you will be starting from there.

Buses

Ecuador has a network of paved roads serving most cities, and distances are generally short, making bus travel quite easy, cheap and convenient. Most intercity buses are modern and fairly comfortable, and you can stop them almost anywhere on the highway (daytime only), although of course it is best to be traveling light. Highway toll stations are a good place to wait. The main downtown Quito bus terminal – the Terminal Terrestre – is useful, but has a bad reputation for theft *(see Crime and Security, page 97)*. All major cities have public bus terminals, which most bus lines use. As a rule of thumb, cost of bus travel is about 1 dollar per hour of travel time.

Left: hotel staff in Lago San Pablo

In Quito, some bus companies have their own terminals in the new city, with first-class direct bus routes, and these are the best option for long-distance travel.

The best-known bus lines serving the major highland and coastal cities are:

Transportes Panamericana, Avenida Colón y Reina Victoria, tel: 257-0900.
Flota Imbabura, Manuel Larrea y Portoviejo, tel: 257-2657.
Trans Esmeraldas, Santa María y 9 de Octubre, tel: 250-5099 (to Lago Agrio and Coca).
Reina del Camino, 18 de Septiembre y Manuel Larrea, tel: 257-2673 (to Manta and Puerto López).

Urban buses are abundant and frequent in the cities, but you have to know the routes. However, in Quito three bus lines that run north–south from the old to new cities on exclusive fast-track lanes are cheap, easy, and even fun to use (but not with baggage, or during crowded peak hours). They also have links to bus services outside the city: the Metrobus, running along Avenida América and Avenida La Prensa; the Trole (electric bus), which runs along 10 de Agosto; and the Ecovía, along 6 de Diciembre.

Airplanes

It takes 8 to 9 hours or more by bus to reach some destinations in the far south, the coast, and the Oriente (such as Cuenca, Loja, Manta, Guayaquil, Lago Agrio, and Coca), and since these are served by reasonably priced air routes, it is often worth saving the time and discomfort by flying.

Galápagos, of course, requires a flight, and these are expensive *(see page 68)*.

The main domestic airlines are:
TAME, Amazonas 13–54 y Colon, tel: 290-9900; www.tame.com.ec
TAME's website is not great, but the airline has a new Airbus fleet for main destinations.
Icaro, Palora 124 y Amazonas, tel: 244-8626 www.icaro.com.ec

If booking well ahead, be sure to reconfirm your reservation at least 24 hours before your flight, or you may get bumped off it.

Taxis

In Quito cabs are cheap, and by law must carry and use a meter. Some drivers will "forget" to switch them on, or claim they are not working. Keep an eye, and settle a price at the outset if there is no meter. The minimum fare is $1, even if the meter reads less. Longer trips, such as a ride into the center from the airport (about $5), tend to be negotiated in advance, without the meter. In Guayaquil and Cuenca, the use of meters is patchy, and it is non-existent elsewhere.

In rural areas, the standard cab is a pick-up truck, and long drives to remote destinations can be expensive, perhaps $20–25 per hour.

Rental Cars

Car rentals are costly (watch out for heavy deductibles), and it is generally cheaper to hire a car with driver, which also relieves you of parking and security headaches. However, rentals are available from the usual international companies:
Hertz, Aeropuerto Mariscal Sucre, tel: 225-4258.
Avis, Avenida Amazonas 3–22, tel: 255-0243.
Budget, Avenida Colón y Amazonas, tel: 223 7026.

Trains

Only three short sections of a once-great railroad system are still running: Ibarra–Primer Paso, Quito–El Boliche (Cotopaxi), and Riobamba–Alausí–Sibambe *(see page 45)*. These are all tourism excursions, and do not serve the function of getting from A to B.

Tricycle Taxis

Motorized tricycle taxis, which can carry a couple of passengers and some baggage, are ubiquitous in coastal and lowland towns. They are a cheap and fun way to get around for short and medium distances.

Bicycles

Not exactly a means of transport in Ecuador, more of a sporting item, but very popular. Mountain-bike rentals and organized cycling excursions can be found in the major centers mentioned. Cotopaxi National Park is a popular biking area.

The following are recommended:
The Biking Dutchman, Foch 714 y Juan León Mera, Quito, tel: 256-8323, www.biking-dutchman.com
Jatun Pacha, Avenida 31 de Octubre 19 y Panamericana, Otavalo, tel: 292-2223.
The Travel Center, Hermano Miguel 4–46 y Larga, Cuenca, tel: 282-3782, www.terradiversa.com/ttc

ACCOMMODATIONS

Quoted prices often do not include the 12 percent tax, plus 10 percent service that the better hotels add to the bill. In low tourism season discounts are fairly easy to negotiate. Many hotels in popular weekend resorts near Quito offer weekday discounts.

Many but not all hotels include a continental breakfast in the quoted room price. Bear in mind that when staying in a rural *hacienda* or lodge you are also obliged to take all your meals there. Some lodges' rates are fully inclusive, but most are not and the additional meal charges will add significantly to the cost of your stay.

Published rates for a standard double, plus tax and service are as follows:

$$$$$ More than $130
$$$$ $90–129
$$$ $35–89
$$ $15–34
$ less than $14

Quito
Old City
Patio Andaluz
García Moreno N6–52 y Mejía
Tel: 228-0830
www.hotelpatioandaluz.com
An upscale hotel in a fine, restored Republican mansion close to the Plaza Indepencia. $$$$

Hotel San Francisco de Quito
Sucre 217 y Guayaquil
Tel: 228-7758
E-mail: hsfquito@andinanet.net
Colonial patio hotel, a bit noisy but good location. $$

The Secret Garden
Antepara E–4–60 y Los Rios
Tel: 295-6704
www.secretgardenquito.com
Backpacker spot, very amiable, and its rooftop restaurant has great views over the old city. $

New City
Hilton Colón Quito
Amazonas 110 y Patria
Tel: 256-0666
www.hilton.com
Splendid luxury hotel in the Mariscal district, with an unbeatable location, overlooking Parque El Ejido. $$$$$

Above: the Rancho Ali Shunga, a set of guesthouse cabins outside Otavalo

practical information

Café Cultura
Robles y Reina Victoria
Tel: 222-4271
www.cafecultura.com
Relaxing atmosphere in former mansion, with gardens and library. Popular with visitors. **$$$/$$$$**

Casa Sol
Calama 127 y 6 de Diciembre
Tel: 223-0798
www.casasol.com
Very pleasant, small, and friendly. **$$$**

Hotel Ambassador
9 de Octubre 1052 y Colón
Tel: 256-1777
www.hotel-ambassador.net
Old-style Quito hotel catering mainly to national clientele, good discounts on posted rates. **$$ / $$$**

Villa Nancy
Carrión 336 y 6 de Diciembre
Tel: 256-3084
www.villa-nancy.com
Small, with a homey atmosphere, and a garden. Well located. Good value. **$$**

La Gasca District
Toa Bed & Breakfast
Lizarazu N23–209 y La Gasca
Tel: 222-4241
www.hostaltoa.ec
Friendly, intimate atmosphere. Very convenient for new cable car station. **$$$**

Mindo Area
Bellavista Cloud Forest Reserve
Tandayapa Valley
Tel: 223-2313 (in Quito)
www.bellavistacloudforest.com
An isolated lodge in the high cloudforest of the Tandayapa valley, with beautiful trails, waterfalls, and bird life. **$$$$**

El Monte
Eastbound Highway, Km3
Tel: 276-5427
www.ecuadorcloudforest.com
A popular eco-lodge outside Mindo near the butterfly farm, with waterfall and spacious grounds for walks. **$$$$** (full board)

Right: patio at Hacienda Cusin, Lago San Pablo

Hacienda San Vicente
Tel: 223-5276 (Quito)
Known as 'The Yellow House,' just out of the center. Family atmosphere, good value. **$$$**

Cabañas Armonía
Tel: 276-5471
www.orchids-birding.com
A secluded little spot a few blocks from the main street, with private cabins amidst orchid gardens. **$$**

Otavalo
Rancho Ali Shungu
www.ranchoalishungu.com
Quiet getaway spot up in the hills, yet only 5km (3 miles) from Otavalo. Has spacious guest houses and spectacular views. Run by the Ali Shungu Foundation for the benefit of the local community. **$$$$$** (includes two meals).

Hacienda Cusín
Lago San Pablo
Tel: 291-8013
www.haciendacusin.com
A classic old *hacienda*, decorated with colonial paintings and antiques. Beautiful grounds. 15 minutes' drive from Otavalo. **$$$$**

Ali Shungu
Calle Quito con M Egas
Tel: 292-0750
www.alishungu.com
Another Ali Shungu Foundation hotel *(see above)*, an elegant, friendly and well-kept place, with a big lawn and flower garden, in the center of Otavalo. Gourmet restaurant. **$$$**

La Casa de Hacienda
Tel: 294-6336
E-mail:
hosteriacasadehacienda@hotmail.com
3km (2 miles) north of Otavalo, just right
of Pan-American highway. A very pleasant
hacienda-style hotel. Good value. **$$$**

Jatun Pacha
Avenida 31 de Octubre 19 y Panamericana
Tel: 292-2223
Clean and friendly garden hotel. **$$**

Papallacta
Hotel Termas de Papallacta
Tel: 256-8989 (Quito)
www.termaspapallacta.com
A comfortable lodge in a beautiful setting
with private thermal pools and a spa. **$$$**

Hostería La Pampa,
Tel: 248-6286
A modest, pleasant hotel near the main
road turn-off to the hot springs. **$$**

Cotopaxi Area
La Cíenega
Tel: Lasso 541-337
Tel: 254-1337 (Quito)
www.geocities.com/haciendaec
One of Ecuador's classic old *haciendas*,
situated 8km (5 miles) south of the main
entrance to the national park. **$$$**

Tambopaxi Acclimatization Center
Tel: 222-0242 (Quito)
www.tambopaxi.com
Situated in the park near the foot of
Cotopaxi. Camping allowed. **$$$** (full
board)

La Estación de Machachi
Aloasí
Tel: 230-9246
Just west of Machachi, this is a family-run
hacienda. Good base for acclimatization
climb of El Corazón. Reservations
required. **$$**

Galápagos
Most people stay on boats while visiting
the Galápagos *(see page 69 for booking
suggestions)*. However, for those planning
to stay in Puerto Ayora the following
hotels are recommended:

Red Mangrove Inn
Avenida Charles Darwin y Las Fragatas
Tel: 252-6564
Luxurious accommodations in beautiful
surroundings, plus a very comprehensive
program of land-based excursions. **$$$$**

Hotel Galápagos
*Avenida Charles Darwin, by entrance to
Darwin Research Station*
Tel: 252-6330
www.hotelgalapagos.com
Seafront hotel on Academy Bay, just
outside Puerto Ayora. It's set within
2 hectares (5 acres) of grounds. **$$$**

Sol y Mar
Tel: 252-6281
An old favorite with travelers: a waterfront
hotel in the center of Puerto Ayora. **$$**

Lirio del Mar
Naveda y Berlanga
Tel: 252-6212
Reasonably priced, this hotel represents
good value, and is just two blocks from
the waterfront. **$**

Baños
Luna Runtun
Tel: 274-0882
www.lunaruntun.com
A very luxurious spa lodge 6km (4 miles)
from Baños, with stupendous views across
the valley and of Tungurahua. Lots of
outdoor activities. **$$$$$**

Monte Selva
Halflants y Montalvo
Tel: 274-0566
E-mail: hmonteselva@hotmail.com
A range of private cabins, located within
spacious grounds. **$$$**

Isla de Baños
Halflants 1–31 y Montalvo
Tel: 274-0609
E-mail: islabaños@andinanet.net
Guests here enjoy the garden setting,
comfortable rooms and Jacuzzi. **$$**

Right: staff at the Hacienda Leito Hotel, near Patate

Plantas y Blanco
Luis Martinez y 12 de Noviembre
Tel: 274-0044
E-mail: option3@hotmail.com
Safe, clean, and friendly hotel with a great rooftop café and steam baths. Varying room prices. Recommended. **$**

Riobamba

Hostería Abraspungo
Km 3.5 Riobamba-Guano highway
Tel: 294-0820
www.abraspungo.com
Lovely *hacienda*-style country house in a beautiful setting close to Riobamba, with a comprehensive range of services. **$$$**

Hotel El Cisne
Daniel Leon Borja y Duchicela
Tel: 296-4573
elcisne@yahoo.com
Large, modern hotel with a sauna/spa, just 10 blocks from the station. **$$$**

Hotel Zeus
Avenida Daniel Leon Borja 41–29
Tel: 296-8036
www.hotelzeus.com.ec
Large, modern, and luxurious, the hotel features interesting cultural objects and superb views. Varying room prices. **$$$**

El Tren Dorado,
Carabobo 22–35 y 10 de Agosto
Tel: 296-4890
E-mail: htrendorado@hotmail.com
Good value, includes breakfast. Very close to station. **$$**

Los Shyris
Rocafuerte 21–60 y 10 de Agosto
Tel: 296-0323/294-6055
E-mail: hshyris@yahoo.com
A good-value option, very close to the station, with a range of services that includes Internet access. **$$**

Cuenca

Hotel El Dorado
Gran Colombia 787 y Luis Cordero
Tel: 283-1390
E-mail: H5113-GM@accor-hotels.com
Luxury hotel with great location, one block from Parque Calderón. Gourmet restaurant with views of cathedral and city. **$$$$**

Hotel Victoria
Calle Larga 6–93 y Borrero
Tel: 282-7401
www.grupo-santaana.com
Elegant new hotel on the *barranco,* in a remodeled mansion with splendid original features, including wood paneling. **$$$**

Posada del Angel
Bolivar 14–11 y Esteves de Toral
Tel: 284-0695
E-mail: posadadelangel@hotmail.com
Old colonial house, with light and airy interior and a nice atmosphere. **$$$**

Hostal Macondo
Calle Tarqui 11–64 y Lamar
Tel: 284-0697
www.macondo.cedei.org
Restored colonial house with garden. Pleasant; recommended. **$$**

Hotel Milan
Presidente Córdova 989 y Padre Aguirre
Tel: 283-1104
Very good value, breakfast included. Some rooms overlook market square; great view from rooftop cafeteria. $

Tinku
Honorato Vásquez 5–66 y Hermano Miguel
Tel: 283-9845
E-mail: tinkuenca@yahoo.es
Intimate, friendly backpacker place. $

Puerto López Area

Hotel Pacífico
Malecón Izurieta y Lascano
Tel: 230-0147
E-mail: hpacific@manta.ecua.net.ec
Right on the promenade in the town center. Swimming pool; varying room rates. $$$

Hostería Alandaluz
Ruta del Sol
Puerto Rico
Tel: 278-0690
www.alandaluz.com
A famous earth-friendly eco lodge on the beach about 15km (12 miles) south of Puerto López, with access to the Cantalapiedra wildlife reserve. $$$

Hostería Mandala
Malecón Izurieta, extremo norte
Tel: 230-0181
www.hosteriamandala.com
Friendly lodge right on the beach, with private cabins in jungly gardens. $$

Hostería La Terraza
Tel/fax: 230-0235
In the hills above town, with views over the bay. Small, very secluded, and peaceful. $$

Hostal Plaza Real
Lascano y Machalilla
Tel: 230-0172
Small, comfortable hotel in town center. $$

Hostal Cueva del Oso
Lascano 116 y Montalvo
Tel: 230-0124
Family hostel, with kitchen available. $

HEALTH & EMERGENCIES

Hygiene/General Health
Bottled water is widely available, and you should drink only that or water known to have been thoroughly boiled. Stay away from uncooked salads, and peel fruit yourself if you can. In general, use your judgment about the cleanliness of a locale.

In case of serious accident or illness advise your embassy, and try to get to Quito or Guayaquil for treatment. It is highly advisable to carry medical insurance, including repatriation cover.

Altitude sickness can be a problem, especially in lofty spots like the Cotopaxi National Park. It's not usually a problem in Quito but drink plenty of fluids, eat lightly, and avoid alcohol and exertion when you first arrive. If planning a serious mountain climb it is vital to acclimatize by ascending gradually and spending time at high altitude beforehand.

Visitors to the Oriente and the north coast should have yellow fever vaccinations. Malaria prophylaxis is also recommended; consult a specialist for options and the latest information. Dengue fever is also a risk in these areas. It exhibits severe flu-like symptoms and lacks either treatment or prophylaxis, but is almost never fatal. It lasts about one week. Generally, remoter areas carry lower risk of infection, due to the scarcity of human vectors. All of the above diseases are transmitted by insect bites, so the use of insect repellent is important. Use a mosquito net while sleeping.

Above: hospitable owners of the Hostería Mandala

Leishmaniasis is a rare but unpleasant disease which is occasionally contracted by travelers to the Oriente. Also transmitted by insect bite, it manifests as a persistent sore or lump where the fly bit. If in doubt, see a tropical medicine specialist.

Medical/Dental Services

Pharmacies are numerous, and sell most medications without a prescription. They will also split up packages and sell pills individually. Check expiry dates.

The following are recommended in Quito:
Hospital Metropolitano
Avenida Mariana de Jesus y Occidental, tel: 226-1520 (information), 226-5020 (emergency and ambulance).
General Practitioners (English-speaking):
Eduardo Larrea
Hospital Metropolitano, Avenida Mariana de Jesús y Occidental, 3rd floor, Office 311, tel: 226-7652 or 09-919-4665
Ramiro Velasco
Acuña 107 y Inglaterra, tel: 222-4084 or 09-947-8096

Vaccinations and laboratory analysis:
Clínica Pichincha
Veintimilla E3–30 y Paez, tel: 256-2296

Dentist (English-speaking):
Silvia Altamirano
Amazonas 32227 y Republica, tel: 224-4119

Crime and Security

Drug and guerrilla problems in Colombia sometimes spill over into Ecuadorean border areas, and in 2000 and 2001 some foreign oil workers and tourists were kidnapped in Sucumbíos. At the time of writing warnings against travel to this and other areas of the Oriente are posted in several consular advisories. However, consulates are always ultra cautious – the same advisories also warn against visiting Baños, despite minimal levels of volcanic activity. Make local inquiries about the current situation before going *(see Useful Addresses, page 98)*.

Be aware that, as a tourist, you are known to be carrying money and valuables, and are the perfect target for thieves. Carry your money and passport in a money pouch worn under your clothes, and don't flaunt expensive jewelry and watches. Be especially careful in crowded places, such as bus terminals and markets, and on urban buses, where you should hug your daypack in front and leave no camera or shoulder bag hanging loose. Watch out for street set-ups, such as a nasty liquid squirted on your clothes or money dropped at your feet; anything that might distract your attention while they rob you.

As a precaution, make photocopies of passport, airline tickets, travelers' checks, and other important documents, and keep them separate from the originals.

The Terminal Terrestre in Quito has a particularly bad reputation for pickpockets and bag slashers, so take great care here, especially if alone. Groups should watch each other's bags and stick together. Get a claim check for baggage placed in the hold.

In big cities, avoid parks and deserted streets during hours of darkness, and use a taxi to get back to your hotel late at night.

Rural areas are the safest, but armed hold-ups and rapes sometimes occur on popular circuits, and you should inquire locally about safety. On the north coast it is not safe to wander off alone on deserted beaches.

Buses are occasionally held up by armed 'passengers,' usually at night. Those first-class services that run at night do security checks on passengers and ban the use of cell phones (used to co-ordinate getaway vehicles) on buses. Always try to travel by day.

Never pay street hustlers for tour services; if they are selling something that sounds interesting, go with them to the agency they claim to represent before paying anything.

COMMUNICATIONS AND NEWS

Internet

The major Ecuadorean cities have numerous internet cafés, with service for about $1.50 per hour. Some of them offer a period of free internet access if you eat there. In the Mariscal district of Quito, the one called Amazonet at Avenida Amazonas N24–84 y Foch is quiet and comfortable and has a relatively fast internet connection. Net-to-phone calls to Europe and North America are widely available and save money.

Mail

Mail services are fairly reliable, but are very expensive. For example, a letter or post-card to Europe currently costs $3. The most efficient and convenient post office in Quito is at Colón y Reina Victoria. It's open Monday to Friday 8am–6pm, and on Saturday 8am–noon.

Telephone & Fax

Public telephone offices, operated by a number of different companies, are plentiful in the big cities, and company-specific phone cards are sold everywhere. Every small town has its public phone office, but you won't always find these remote villages. Note that when using public telephones you must always dial the area code even for local calls in the same area.

Ecuador's International code: 593
(omit initial 0 from area code)
To call abroad: 00
(omit initial 0 from area code)
Information: 100
Local operator: 105
International operator: 116

Area Codes for places in this book:
Quito (Pichincha) 02
Guayaquil (Guayas) 04
Galápagos 05
Puerto López (Manabí) 05
Cuenca (Azuay) 07
Cotopaxi (Cotopaxi) 03
Baños (Tungurahua) 03
Esmeraldas (Esmeraldas) 06
Otavalo (Imbabura) 06
Tena (Napo) 06
All cell phones 09

Media

CNN is available on the local cable channel, which most big-city hotels will have, at least in the lobby. News magazines and some international newspapers may be found at newsstands outside the big hotels.

USEFUL ADDRESSES

South American Explorers
Jorge Washington 311 y Leonidas Plaza, Quito
Tel/fax: 222-5228
www.saexplorers.org
A valuable resource for independent travelers. The annual membership fee of $50, which probably pays for itself in money saved and rip-offs avoided, includes a subscription to the quarterly magazine, access to the clubhouse, with books, maps, trip reports, and a library; luggage storage; widespread member discounts; opportunities to meet other travelers and organize groups for Galápagos tours, climbing etc; latest information on crime, safety, danger areas, etc. Highly recommended.

Tour Operators

Quito
Safari
Foch E5–39
Tel: 255-2505 (toll-free from the US & Canada: 1-800-434-8182)
www.safari.com.ec
Broad range of itineraries in adventure travel and Galápagos bookings. Owner Jean Brown (available on weekends) is a mine of information on all things Ecuadorean. Open seven days a week.

Andando Tours
Avenida Coruña N25–311 y Orellana
Tel: 255-0952
www.angermeyercruises.com
Operate some of the nicest small cruise boats
in Galápagos.
Explorandes
Presidente Wilson 537 y Diego de Almagro
Tel: 222-6999
www.explorandes.com
River rafting and kayaking a specialty.
Metropolitan Touring
Avenida República de El Salvador N36–84
y Naciones Unidas
Tel: 298-8200
www.metropolitan-touring.com
The Big Daddy of Ecuadorean tour opera-
tors, with itineraries throughout the country.
Runs large cruise ships in Galápagos.
Biking Dutchman
Foch 714 y Juan León Mera
Tel: 254-2806
www.biking-dutchman.com
Well-known and reliable service for mountain-
biking tours.

Cuenca
The Travel Center
Hermano Miguel 4–46 y Larga
Tel: 282-3782
www.terradiversa.com/ttc
Three tour operators offering various tours.

Puerto López
Machalilla Tours
Malecón Izurieta
Tel: 230-0206
machalillatours@yahoo.com
Whale-watching, kayak, snorkeling; tours to
Isla de la Plata and Machalilla National Park.

Embassies & Consulates

(all in Quito)
Canada: Avenida 6 de Diciembre 2816 y
Paul Rivet, Edificio Josueth Gonzalez,
4th floor, tel: 223-2114
Denmark: República de El Salvador 733
y Portugál, Edificio Gabriela 3, 3rd floor,
tel: 243-7163
France: General Leonidas Plaza 107 y
Patria, tel: 256-0789
Germany: Edificio Citiplaza, Avenida
Naciones Unidas y República de El

Salvador, tel: 297-0820
Ireland: Antonio de Ulloa 2651, tel:
245-1577
Israel: Eloy Alfaro 969 y Amazonas,
tel: 256-5509
Italy: La Isla 111 y Humberto Albornoz,
tel: 256-1074
The Netherlands: Avenida 12 de Octubre
1942 y Cordero Building, tel: 222-9229
Sweden & Norway: Avenida República
de El Salvador N34–39, tel: 227-8189
Switzerland: Juan Pablo Sanz y Avenida
Amazonas 3617, tel: 243-4949
UK: Edificio Citiplaza, Avenida Naciones
Unidas y República de El Salvador, tel:
297-0800
USA: Avenida Patria y Avenida 12 de
Octubre, tel: 256-2890

LANGUAGE

Spanish is a fairly easy language, but under-
standing street Spanish is another matter.
Many people, particularly in tourism services, speak a little English and love to practice it. You will not need Quichua, except
in very remote highland areas.

A few phrases to keep you out of trouble:
Si, No Yes, No
Por favor Please
Gracias Thank you
A la orden At your service, think nothing
of it
Buenos días Good morning
Buenas tardes/noches Good afternoon/
evening, night
Disculpe Excuse me
Hola Hello
Adios/Hasta Luego Goodbye/see you later
Cuanto? How much?
Cuando? When?
Donde? Where?
Porque Why?/Because
La cuenta The bill
Yo quisiera I would like to
Tengo sed I'm thirsty
Tengo hambre I'm hungry
Policía de turismo Tourist police
Aeropuerto Airport
Terminal terrestre Bus station
Playa Beach
Iglesia Church

Left: mail drop-off and pick-up at Post Office Bay, Floreano, Galápagos

ACKNOWLEDGEMENTS

All Photography   **Peter Frost** *except*
10   **Brooklyn Museum of Art/Corbis**
11   **AKG-images/London/Veintimalla**
12, 14, 15   **Mary Evans Picture Library**
13   **AKG-images London**
16   **Reuters/Corbis**
30   *courtesy of* **Bellavista Cloud Forest Reserve**
54   **Yadid Levy/alamy**
55   **Pablo Corral V/Corbis**
Front cover   **Paul Harris/Stone/Getty Images**

Original Cartography   **Mapping Ideas Ltd**
Additional Cartography   **Mike Adams and James Macdonald**

INDEX

Guayaquil 12, 13, 17, 39, 53, 56
Guayaquil–Quito railroad 14, 17
Guayasamín, Oswaldo 22, 25
Gutierrez, President Lucio 16, 17

Health 63, 88, 96–7
history 11–17
Huaorani, the 65
Humboldt, Alexander von 12, 17

Incas, the 11, 12, 13, 21, 31, 32, 34, 39, 47, 48, 50, 51, 59
Ingapirca 39, 47–8
indigenous peoples 11, 15, 16, 17, 21, 24, 27, 31, 32, 47, 50, 53, 54, 56, 59, 61, 63, 64, 65, 75
Isabela, Galápagos 70
Isinliví 40
Isla de la Plata 57, 58–9
Itualo 41

Jipijapa 61

Lago Agrio 64
Lago San Pablo 33
language 99
Las Vegas culture 55
Latacunga 39
La Tola 54
La Tolita 11, 17
La Tortugita 61
Los Frailes 61
Llanganates National Park 39
Lloa 35
Loja 11

Machachi 35, 36
Machala 53
Machalilla National Park 58, 60
Mahuad, President Jamil 15, 16, 17
Manglaralto 56
Manta 53, 55
Manta culture 17
Manteños, the 11, 55, 59, 61
Manto de la Novia falls 45
markets 32, 40, 49, 57, 76, 77
Mindo 21, 28
Mindo Butterfly Farm 29
Mindo-Nambillo Reserve 29–30
Misahuallí 65
Mitad del Mundo 21, 26, 27, 28
Montañita 55, 58
Montecristi 55, 61

Montuvio coast 54–5
Mount Cotopaxi 12
Muisne 54
museums
    Archeological Museum (Agua Blanca) 61
    Balseros del Mar del Sur (Salango) 59
    Folk Art Museum (Guayasamín) 25
    Inti Ñan Museum 27
    Museo de las Culturas Aborígenes
        (Cuenca) 50, 77
    Museo de las Conceptas (Riobamba) 46
    Museo del Banco Central (Cuenca) 50
    Museo del Banco Central (Manta) 55
    Museo del Banco Central de la Reserva
        (Quito) 24
    Museo de los Amantes de Sumpa
        (Santa Elena) 56
    Museum of Modern Art (Cuenca) 49
    Museo Real Alto (Chanduy) 56
    Solar Culture Museum 27
    Whale Muscum (Puerto López) 57

Nambillo waterfalls 30
Nanegalito 30
nightlife 82–3
Noboa, Gustavo 16
Nono 28

Oil 15, 16, 17, 29, 53, 63, 64, 65
Olón 55
Orellana, Francisco de 12, 17
Oriente, El 15, 63–5
Otavalo 21, 31–3, 76

Pailón del Diablo falls 44, 45
Palacio, Alfredo 16, 17
Paltas, the 11
Panama hats 51, 55, 61, 75, 77
Papallacta 21, 37
Parque Bolívar 56
Pastaza 42, 43, 45
Peguche 33, 76
Peru 11, 14, 15, 17
Pichincha volcano 17, 21
Pile 61
Pizarro, Francisco 12, 17
Planetarium 27
Playa Arena Negra 61
Playas 56
population 89
Post Office Bay, Galápagos 70
Protocol of Rio de Janeiro 15
Puerto Cayo 61